"The goal of most leaders is to cause people to feel reverence for the leader...

The goal of the EXCEPTIONAL LEADER is to cause people to feel reverence for themselves".

CHRISTOPHER J. HEGARTY

# 7 SECRETS
# OF
# EXCEPTIONAL LEADERSHIP

**A SELF-DIRECTED PROGRAM
DESIGNED TO HELP YOU QUICKLY EVALUATE AND DEVELOP
YOUR LEADERSHIP SKILLS**

**CHRISTOPHER J. HEGARTY**                    **PHILIP B. NELSON**

**NEW EXPANDED EDITION**

Dedicated to:

**MAHREN CAHLIL MICHAEL**

And

**MICHAEL MIKE, SR. And THOMAS PATRIC**

## ACKNOWLEDGMENTS

A very special thanks to Sally Hudson who organized, focused, and edited this edition.

Cover design by Nancy Olbers

Thanks to Sandra Orchid, Patricia Page, Chandler Peterson, and Samantha Spade for their insightful comments about this edition

Thanks to Frank Ciccarelli, Ted Helberg, Jim Liautaud, Arleen Olson, Thomas Patric, Duke Rudman, and Lou Witt who assisted in developing the original manuscript.

# TABLE OF CONTENTS

# INTRODUCTION

The *7 Secrets of Exceptional Leadership* learning program is a collaboration: the evaluation portion was written by Nelson; the text was written by Hegarty.

In our work as speakers, trainers, and consultants to many of the world's major corporations (as well as many other large and small organizations) Phil Nelson and I have had the long-term opportunity to research and identify the skills that consistently exceptional leaders have in common. While there are numerous areas where leaders must excel, we have identified ones we believe are most critical. These secrets of exceptional leadership are:

- ◆ *VISION*
- ◆ *EXECUTION*
- ◆ *INSPIRATION*
- ◆ *DRIVE*
- ◆ *OWNERSHIP*
- ◆ *EMPATHY*

## *DEVOTION*
In addition to the six secrets of leadership listed above there is a seventh secret that is equal to or more valuable than any of the others. It is lifelong DEVOTION to improving competence in every area of leadership. *It underscores and integrates all the aspects of being an exceptional leader.*

*7 Secrets of Exceptional Leadership* is a program for evaluating and continuously developing your leadership skills. We begin by providing a context for today's exceptional leader, setting the stage for why the skills we've identified are so critical. Next is a self-assessment to evaluate your leadership ability along these skill dimensions. This evaluation is your leadership profile and provides a benchmark for developing these critical leadership skills. Lastly, we discuss a variety of change strategies to provide guidance along your development journey.

*The principles herein are applicable to the exceptional leadership of a family, country, business, religion, or social group.*

**Please cover the rest of this page and read only one question at a time:**

1. Have you ever been, are you now, or do you plan to be in the future, involved in a major league vitally important position of leadership? Yes_____ No_____.
2. Have you ever been, are you now, or do you plan to be in the future, involved in the raising of children? Yes_____ No_____.
3. Please reread question 1 and answer it again.

In our seminars, less than 5% of the participants' answer yes to question 1 the first time and over 90% answer yes the second time. The most vital leadership role, for most of us, is the raising of our family. Yet, we tend to trivialize our most important leadership responsibility and make others seem more important. This quiz also proves most people do not see themselves in significant positions of leadership in their work. Without a strong vision of becoming an exceptional leader you will almost certainly not become one.

# WHAT YOU SEIZE IS WHAT YOU GET

## How To Get Maximum Value From This Learning Program!

**VIP:** Apply INTENTION to your ATTENTION - do not just read - decide with high intention what you will do to refine your skills.

It is in covering material for the first time that you are most likely to get insights about how to capitalize on what you are learning. This program has been written in workbook format leaving a blank page across from each page of text to allow you to record your thoughts, questions and plans about how you will employ the material.

## Seize the opportunity!

1) Do not skim or speed read. Investing your undivided attention in what you are doing will dramatically increase the value you receive from this program

2) Review all this material in depth with full attention in an environment where you will not be distracted or disturbed.

3) Give very careful thought to how to capitalize on the ideas and strategies.

4) Record all the thoughts that come to your mind and all the plans that you make on the blank pages across from the text.

5) Be sure to date all your notes for further review.

You are joining many thousands of men and women who have found *7 Secrets of Leadership* to be a valuable and practical tool to increase their competence.

We will remind you several times during this program to reflect on how effectively you are following the guidelines to derive maximum value from the program.

## Remember, what you seize is what you get!

# EVALUATING YOUR CURRENT LEADERSHIP SKILLS

# Welcome

You are joining many thousands of individuals who have utilized this learning program to develop their leadership skills Your path to exceptional leadership starts with an assessment of your skill level in vision, execution, inspiration, drive, ownership, and empathy. This provides you with a benchmark to continuously improve as an exceptional leader.

### A SELF DIRECTED EVALUATION *

The assessment enables you to 1) evaluate your current leadership competence along six major skill dimensions 2) understand each of these dimensions 3) develop a strategy for increasing your competence in the areas you choose to develop (the seventh skill dimension).

To achieve the greatest benefit from the program, it is not required that you be at the highest level of competency in all of the six areas, but is essential that you:

◆ Recognize where you now stand in each of the six dimensions.

◆ Create a lifelong plan to continuously expand your mastery of them.

◆ Back yourself up with the appropriate talent and strength in your organization by hiring people who are strong where you are not.

### REVIEW PERIODICALLY . . .
### APPLY WHAT YOU LEARN . . .
### AND CHART YOUR PROGRESS

You can make rapid strides in creating new levels of competence and flexibility in yourself and your people. This is vital in a world that is changing at ever increasing, blinding rates of speed.

*_After completing and applying the information in the program,_ if you would like to take the evaluation a second time to assess your improvement in leadership skills, please send us your written comments about the program, along with a self-addressed, stamped envelope to the address below and we'll send one to you, free of charge.

**Institute for Exceptional Performance**
**P.O. Box 1152, Novato, CA 94948  USA**
**Telephone (415) 892-2858**
**e-mail:** leaders@cutting-edge.com

# DIRECTIONS

I. YOUR CURRENT LEADERSHIP SELF-EVALUATION – You will find the evaluation in the back of this book
    A.       Take it when you will not be interrupted or distracted.
    B.       Read each statement carefully and decide whether or not it applies to you.
    C.       If a statement is true, circle the "T" next it. If a statement is false, circle the "F." If you are uncertain, answer in the direction that *most* applies to you.
    D.       Be ruthlessly truthful if you want an accurate score; there are no "right" or "wrong answers."
    **E.**       **This questionnaire can be distorted. Answer the questions in regard to how you currently *are*, not how you would like to be. *This is very important.***

II. RECORD AND REVIEW THE RESULTS
    A.       After you have responded to each statement, separate the pages of the test.
    B.       Tally the number of Vs circled. Enter the total in the appropriate space.
    C.       Use the same procedure to count and record the results for **E, I, D, O,** and **M.**
    D.       Transfer all totals V-M to the appropriate blank on the profile sheet.

III. COMPLETING YOUR LEADERSHIP EVALUATION

Plot each of your scores V-M into the appropriate profile graph by drawing a line across the graph level with your score.

IV. MEASURING YOUR SELF-EVALUATION

After you have completed your self-evaluation, study the remainder of the program. Record thoughts, questions, concerns, etc. on the worksheet page opposite each page of text. Then begin to apply the material carefully and use it to develop your leadership competence.

V. USING THE PROGRAM ON AN ONGOING BASIS

Periodically review your progress. Take the evaluation again. (See page 66 for information on how to obtain another assessment.) This will enable you to continuously review your progress. Create a blueprint for the changes that you choose to make, then execute your plan. There are exercises to do in each area and recommended readings to help you on your way. Review your program regularly. And whenever appropriate, get feedback from people around you to see if the intended changes are actually happening.

**The evaluation is for your personal use. There is no need to send it to us. It is designed to help you gain insight. It is not designed to be used in selection, or in predicting a person's future leadership success.**

1. People might describe me as impractical . . . . . . . . . .     T    F
2. I frequently procrastinate on things I dislike . . . . . . . .     T    F
3. I find it hard, at times, to clearly explain to others my point of view     T    F
4. I find it easy to relax and completely forget my work     T    F
5. I know if I commit to it, I can accomplish anything I set my mind to . . . . . . . . . . . .     T    F
6. I find it easy to build meaningful, deep friendships     T    F
7. I have missed opportunities that I should have seen . . .     T    F
8. I have always worked, even when I was in school . . . .     T    F
9. People have always listened to me . . . . . . . . . . . . . .     T    F
10. I always seem to have several things going at the same time     T    F
11. People who achieve financial success generally have had the right "breaks" . . . . . . . .     T    F
12. I don't always "read" people well . . . . . . . . . . . . . .     T    F
13. I always seem to have a good "sense" of what will work     T    F
14. I have good ideas but, at times, I can't seem to muster the extra effort to act on them     T    F
15. People would consider me to be rather quiet . . . . . . . .     T    F
16. I find it hard to get going again after I've failed at something . . . . . . . . . .     T    F
17. The income I can earn and success I can achieve is unlimited . . . . . . . . . . .     T    F
18. I find I am interested in and have relationships with a broad range of people . . .     T    F
19. I often have more ideas than time to deal with them . . .     T    F
20. I am one who generally plans things well in advance . . .     T    F
21. I enjoy speaking in front of a group and seek out the opportunity to do so . . . . .     T    F
22. It seems that I never have enough time to accomplish all of the things that I would like     T    F
23. At times I feel I am not talented enough to accomplish my objectives . . . . . . . .     T    F
24. If people are left alone on the job they will often slack off     T    F
25. I generally have a very good feel for how things will turn out in the future . . . . . .     T    F
26. I am not always dependable     T    F
27. I would probably not be highly successful in sales . . . . . .     T    F
28. Relative to other things in my life, I find that I really don't enjoy my work . . . . . . .     T    F
29. Whatever happens to me, good or bad, I know I made the decisions and was in control     T    F

30. I openly express what I feel, good and bad . . . . . . . .     T    F
31. I can have difficulty "seeing" things clearly in my mind . . .     T    F
32. I am well organized in nearly everything I do . . . . . . . . .     T    F
33. I am very good at "moving" people toward my point of view     T    F
34. I often feel that I am not as successful as I could be     T    F
35. I have had periods of "bad luck"     T    F
36. I am better at getting things done than in understanding people .     T    F
37. Overall, I am more practical than creative . . . . . . . . . . . . .     T    F
38. I generally perform best in a crisis . . . . . . . . . . . . . .     T    F
39. I have held many offices in organizations . . . . . . . . . .     T    F
40. I rarely become impatient with delays or interruptions . . . . .     T    F
41. I have several goals that I have set for myself and I am working on currently . . . . . . . . .     T    F
42. People would describe me as firm but also as very positive .     T    F
43. I often have periods of fantasy and daydreaming . . . . . . . .     T    F
44. I struggle making decisions more than I should at times . . . . . .     T    F
45. I am generally very confident and expressive with regard to my opinions . . . . . . . . . . . .     T    F
46. People would describe me as being totally engrossed in my work . . . . . . . . . . . . . .     T    F
47. I'm not sure what I really want out of life . . . . . . . . . . .     T    F
48. People have told me that I can be insensitive at times . . . . . . .     T    F
49. I really prefer to deal with facts more than ideas . . . . . . . . .     T    F
50. I rarely have trouble with self-discipline . . . . . . . . . . . . .     T    F
51. I am not one who likes to be at the center of attention . . . . .     T    F
52. I really don't enjoy my work as much as I would like . . . . . .     T    F
53. I have often thought I would rather work for myself than for a larger company . . . . . . . . .     T    F
54. I am known for selecting good people and building strong teams     T    F
55. I have had several periods of significant creativity . . . . . . .     T    F
56. I can move too quickly and act impulsively at times . . . . . .     T    F
57. I consider myself to be a very effective communicator . . . . . .     T    F
58. I thrive on challenging situations, the more the better . . . . . . .     T    F
59. My childhood left me ill equipped, in many ways, to deal with life's challenges . . . . . .     T    F
60. Most people who have worked for me have not changed much in their work approach or behavior patterns . . . . . . . . . . . . .     T    F
61. I prefer to analyze decisions carefully rather than trusting my "gut feel" . . . . . . . . . .     T    F

62. I am willing to take calculated risks . . . . . . . . . . . . . .     T    F
63. I am not one who likes to "manipulate" people, even in a positive sense . . . . . . . . .     T    F
64. I find I value my weekends more than my time at work . .     T    F
65. It is clear where I am headed in my career . . . . . . . . . . .     T    F
66. Good performance is easier for me to achieve than good "teamwork" . . . . . . . . . . .     T    F
67. At times I become totally obsessed with an idea and can't seem to let go of it . . . . . .     T    F
68. Once I have solved a problem mentally, I can get bored with implementing a solution . . .     T    F
69. I will often argue the opposite point of view in order to stimulate discussion . . . . . .     T    F
70. I probably shouldn't work so hard but something drives me on . . . . . . . . . . . . . . .     T    F
71. I have been in companies or have had bosses who I feel have held me back . . . . . . . . .     T    F
72. Sometimes I feel I care more about results than people . .     T    F
73. I prefer the tangible to the theoretical and abstract . . . .     T    F
74. I tend to work in "spurts" . .     T    F
75. I am not as good at thinking "on my feet" as in private . .     T    F
76. It is difficult to figure out what truly make me happy . . . . .     T    F
77. I write many of my goals out along with a plan for achieving them . . . . . . . . . . . . . .     T    F
78. People often seek me out for counsel and support on business and personal matters . . . . .     T    F
79. People consider me to be shrewd . . . . . . . . . . . . .     T    F
80. I dislike details . . . . . . . . .     T    F
81. I have been described by many people as charismatic . . . . .     T    F
82. Much of my satisfaction and reward comes from my work     T    F
83. Many times I feel I have had little to do with the "bottom line" results my company or organization has achieved . .     T    F
84. I am not always a good listener     T    F
85. Many of my ideas have become reality . . . . . . . . . . . . . .     T    F
86. I am a person who gets things done, even things I don't like to do . . . . . . . . . . . . . . .     T    F
87. I prefer to think through solutions alone rather than with a group . . . . . . . . . . . . .     T    F
88. I find that I am challenged by accomplishing things that others have given up on . . . . . .     T    F
89. I have thought about starting a small business or buying a franchise . . . . . . . . . . . .     T    F
90. I am very good at developing people that work for me and really enjoy it . . . . . . . . .     T    F

| 1. | V | | 30. | M | | 62. | E | |
| 2. | E | | 31. | V | | 63. | I | |
| 3. | I | | 32. | E | | 64. | D | |
| 4. | D | | 33. | I | | 65. | O | |
| 5. | O | | 34. | D | | 66. | M | |
| 6. | M | | 35. | O | | 67. | V | |
| 7. | V | | 36. | M | | 68. | E | |
| 8. | E | | 37. | V | | 69. | I | |
| 9. | I | | 38. | E | | 70. | D | |
| 10. | D | | 39. | I | | 71. | O | |
| 11. | O | | 40. | D | | 72. | M | |
| 12. | M | | 41. | O | | 73. | V | |
| 13. | V | | 42. | M | | 74. | E | |
| 14. | E | | 43. | V | | 75. | I | |
| 15. | I | | 44. | E | | 76. | D | |
| 16. | D | | 45. | I | | 77. | O | |
| 17. | O | | 46. | D | | 78. | M | |
| 18. | M | | 47. | O | | 79. | V | |
| 19. | V | | 48. | M | | 80. | E | |
| 20. | E | | 49. | V | | 81. | I | |
| 21. | I | | 50. | E | | 82. | D | |
| 22. | D | | 51. | I | | 83. | O | |
| 23. | O | | 52. | D | | 84. | M | |
| 24. | M | | 53. | O | | 85. | V | |
| 25. | V | | 54. | M | | 86. | E | |
| 26. | E | | 55. | V | | 87. | I | |
| 27. | I | | 56. | E | | 88. | D | |
| 28. | D | | 57. | I | | 89. | O | |
| 29. | O | | 58. | D | | 90. | M | |
| | | | 59. | O | | | | |
| | | | 60. | M | | | | |
| | | | 61. | V | | | | |

# YOUR LEADERSHIP PROFILE

Your leadership profile is obtained by transferring each of your scores V through M onto the graphs that correspond to the key skill dimensions on the next page. Indicate your level of development by drawing a line across the graph at the level of your score.

Higher scores indicate that your competency in this area is more developed, whereas lower scores indicate a greater need for development.

Development along any skill dimension, however, is an ongoing and unending process for the exceptional leader. Regardless of the scores, there is always room to grow.

Remember the seventh key leadership dimension: relentless devotion to improving your competency. This is the most vital factor in developing yourself into an exceptional leader.

# NEVER DELUDE YOURSELF THAT YOU KNOW ENOUGH.

*Ignorance, unlike stupidity, can be corrected...but seldom is.*

The single most prominent ingredient in most of history's great leaders is the life-long commitment they had to improving. Greatness in a leader is the result of relentless study and practice. For many, it is not a lack of ability, but a lack of devotion that prevents them from being exceptional leaders.

International human performance consultants and trainers, Leslie and Michael Avery, state *"Never before in history has continuous learning been as vital and urgent. To prosper and grow in this time, it is necessary to surrender many of our beliefs, attitudes and strategies and learn wholly new ways to function. Nothing less will allow a person to become and remain **omnicompetent**."*(See pg. 36)

A savvy executive hired a new employee. On the first morning the new hire reported for work the executive handed him a broom and said *"I like my people to learn this business from the ground up. I'd like you to begin today by sweeping the work area."* The new employee was offended. He said *"What! You want me to sweep the work area? I have a graduate degree in management from a famous university."* The executive responded *"Oh, that's right ... I should have known. Give me the broom and I'll show you how to sweep the work area."*

---

**EACH OF US MUST PREPARE TO DO WORK IN THE FUTURE FOR WHICH NONE OF OUR PRESENT SKILLS MAY BE APPLICABLE.**

---

Many entering the work force now will have to be totally retrained 5 to 7 times in their lifetime.

# LEADERSHIP PROFILE

DEVELOPING COMPETENCY

15
14
13
12
11
10
9
8
7
6
5
4
3
2
1

High

Average

Low

UNDEVELOPED COMPETENCY

VISION    V _____ (score)

EXECUTION    E _____ (score)

INSPIRATION    I _____ (score)

DRIVE    D _____ (score)

OWNERSHIP    O _____ (score)

EMPATHY    M _____ (score)

ii

**DIRECTIONS:** Transfer each of your scores V through M onto the graphs above. Indicate your level of development by drawing a line across the graph at the level of your score.

Higher scores indicate that the competency is more developed, whereas lower scores indicate a greater need for development. Development along any dimension, however, is an *ongoing* and *unending* process for the CONSISTENTLY EXCEPTIONAL LEADER. Regardless of the scores, there is always room to grow. Interpretations of each category are summarized on page four.

# THE EXCEPTIONAL LEADER

## THE NEW ORDER: CHANGE

### *We are in a race that has no finish line.*

**Destructuring is not always destructive.** There should be no doubt in your mind about the accelerating rate of change. Almost half of all the change in the history of the recorded world has happened since 1940. By the year 2000 more than half of all the change in the history of the recorded world will have taken place since 1940. During the 313 days the Cosmonauts were stranded in space (while the Soviet Union was disassembling) more change happened in the world than in some entire centuries. Take a look at the accelerating rate of change in technology. It took decades for the telephone to have a million users, less than 15 years for TV, 5 years for cellular phones and only 4 for PCs. On-line software information systems are the most phenomenal of all, by the year 2000 there will likely be over 30 million on-line subscribers. By comparison, it took more than a century for the Wall Street Journal to acquire 2 million subscribers.

All across America, cutting through every business and profession, the rate of change is exponential. Many organizations are downsizing. Public utilities are required to prove their ability to perform or subcontract their services; the Federal government is talking about reinventing the way it does business to simplify things; companies long known for their lifetime employment, such as IBM, now openly lay off employees. The Sears catalog, once a mainstay of American business culture, is defunct. More and more organizations are hiring top leaders, untried and inexperienced in their industry because of their universal leadership and management talents. It is often necessary because long-standing leaders within the organization are unwilling or unable to make the changes required.

The concept of a fully penetrated market is no longer valid. The Chrysler minivan, the Ford Explorer, Dockers from Levi Strauss, and Staples office supply are prime examples of this fact.

Is this change going to end some time in the future? Almost certainly not. A recent Gallup poll indicates that American business leaders aren't well prepared to take the drastic steps that the changes in the market place demand. The survey, based on a poll of 400 executives from large manufacturing and service companies, found that almost 80% of them view the rate of change in their companies as rapid or extremely rapid. Over 65% of them agree that the rate of change in their companies is likely to accelerate. Despite this, more than half of them said that their firms have no formal structure or clear cut ideas about how to handle change. Those surveyed said the fastest changing areas are cost pressures, information technology, government regulation, customer demands, quality programs, quality achievement of workers and automation. Over two-thirds of the executives in the poll recognize that change is "a threat, and at the same time an opportunity." There are some shining examples of companies (of all sizes) that are adept at continuously managing change, yet, the majority of organizations have proven to be ineffective at doing it.

## SURVIVAL IS A MAJOR CONTRIBUTOR TO LONGEVITY

**Leadership today demands a new skill set; it requires leaders to be in a perpetual state of readiness, immediately prepared to make any and all necessary changes.** Whereas *vision, execution, inspiration, drive, ownership, empathy*, and *devotion* have always been key leadership skills, their importance takes on survival status in today's environment.

John Renesch, editor of New *Traditions in Business* states, *"In these days of constant and profound change, new leadership strategies are being called for--leaders who understand how to inspire rather than control--who are challenged and energized by new leadership requirements, not threatened by them. New leadership strengths must emerge from all levels if an organization is going to survive in this time of downsizing and perpetual reorganizing."*

## TEACHER AND TEAM BUILDER

*"Authoritarian leaders who lay down the law without being open and responsive to others are creating their own demise."*
*Thomas Patric, business advisor*

It might be said that **"Leadership is dead . . . Long live leadership."** The leaders who required blind obedience to their ways of doing things are being replaced by leaders who realize that to succeed today requires the intelligent and wholehearted participation of everybody in the group. In many cases, the changes necessary are more of a challenge for top management than for the rest of the work force. It is no longer enough for a leader to tell people what changes have to be made and why it is necessary . . . the leader today must teach people how to change, what it means to them, and model the needed behavior.

*Chief Executive* Magazine claims the CEO of today must be a team builder, good communicator, able to cope with change, and grasp technical concepts. The CEO of tomorrow must also be ethical, responsive to social, political and environmental forces, have superb judgment and take prudent risks.

Exceptional leaders are often the ones who give birth to an organization, creating its vision, and using superb communication skills to create other *co-visionaries.* Together, they then create the strategies to turn this *co-created* vision into a masterfully executed success. These leaders generate and maintain long-term support, build a team and involve the team members in such a way that they accept responsibility for creating the outcome the organization seeks.

We are clearly differentiating and focusing on leadership as opposed to focusing on the basic dimensions of management such as budgeting, administration, etc. While many management tasks can be automated there will never be a way to automate the leaders participation. Financial consultant Valrie Joy Williams explains it this way, *"Leadership sets the destination--management furnishes transportation for the trip."*

*No organization is big enough or small enough to avoid ever increasing competition.* There is nowhere to hide. The rapidly changing world reveals a leader to his or her people. A major reason good people leave organizations is lack of rapport with their boss. To keep the people you value most requires a high level of rapport and trust between the leader and the people.

Management consultant Eddie Oliver notes, *"The more a leader attempts to hide his/her weaknesses, the more they will negatively affect the performance of the group. Conversely, the more a leader does not try to conceal his/her weaknesses, the less impact they have on team members."*
Exceptional leaders surround themselves with people that are capable in areas where they are not.

# LEADERSHIP: NOT LIMITED TO LEADERSHIP POSITIONS

*"A leader's role is to teach everyone in the organization to be devoted to his/her work.
The leader must lead first.  All employees have to see themselves as executives."*
*Peter Drucker, author of Post Capitalist Society*

**Being a manager does not make you a leader . . .  not being a manager does not prevent you from being a leader . . .  many exceptional leaders are in non-management positions.**  A number of organizations have had major successes because of exceptional individuals who learned how to sell important ideas to others in the group.  Many organizations have been markedly influenced by people who demonstrate leadership qualities but who are not formally in charge of other people as well as by the performance of managers who are not in the top echelon of management.  In *Real Change Leaders*, author Jon Katzenbach gives a number of examples of extraordinary leadership by middle managers.

Warren Gregory, a divisional manager of a large financial services company was such an exceptional leader the entire company (162 divisions) followed his lead.  His division was 146th in economic potential and should have placed very low in performance. However, because his division ranked number one consistently, his innovative leadership was impossible to ignore.  The entire firm, reluctantly at first, and then wholeheartedly, embraced his strategies, taught them to all divisions and increased the productivity of the entire firm.

*Identifying and rewarding both non-management and management leadership increases innovation, productivity, and bottom-line performance.*

## THE SEVENTH SECRET: DEVOTION TO LIFE LONG LEARNING

You did not learn everything you needed to know in kindergarten or in high school or in college or in graduate school.  You will not know what you need to know next year unless you continuously learn how to increase your skills. If you choose to "retire on active duty" you will--by  default--not be an exceptional leader.

Eric Hoffer, the late longshoreman/philosopher described the difference between a learning and a learned society. He explained that, *"In a learning society, people are open to change, willing to try new things, constantly evaluating different approaches, and eagerly approach change and improvement in what they do, seeking to better their understanding of every area of their life. On the other hand, in a learned society, people are convinced they have the answers, are not open to change, resist anybody's attempt to change them, and often become arrogant in the defense of their beliefs and approaches."*

The same could be said about a person. Learning people are always open to change, humble about their current level of knowledge, seek to understand and improve their ability on an ongoing basis. They seek continual new information, attempt always to integrate and improve what they've learned, and are devoted to learning on a life-long basis. On the other hand, learned people have determined that what they have learned is sufficient and close their minds; they stop innovating and searching for new ideas, and they become defensive of anybody or anything that challenges what they believe or do.

The Art of Goal Setting

*Exceptional leaders thrive on continuously developing themselves and others.* They are always improving their competence and the competence of everyone in the group. They are lifelong learners with clear professional and personal goals that they monitor, change and update continuously. (See Ownership section for more on goal setting.)

The risks regarding goals are: 1) not to have any, and 2) to be unwilling to change goals once set. **Goal setting is a never-ending process. Goals once set are to be modified as realities change.** *Persist . . . do not Perseverate.* Ask yourself *"what is the quality of my ongoing learning?"*

♦ *What have I learned in the last year to increase my bottom line performance?*

♦ *What do I plan to learn in the next year to further improve my bottom line performance?*

*Top performers are lifelong learners!* I recently spoke to the top 1/10 of 1% of all insurance agents worldwide at the annual MDRT Top of The Table conference. Even though they are already at the very top of their profession, they remain totally devoted to learning ever better ways. For example, they are using the latest breakthroughs in information technology, which has provided a entirely new way for them to market and improve customer service.

President Teddy Roosevelt visited Chief Justice Oliver Wendell Holmes at home on his 90th birthday. Finding Holmes busy in his study he asked what he was doing. Holmes replied *"Keeping up on my studies . . . I am learning the Greek language."* What a great example of a lifelong learner.

*Many individuals have retired on active duty and have stopped learning.* They mistakenly hope that their formal education, past successes, tenure, etc. will safeguard their position. Ironically, this is most prevalent in America's educational system. A number of forward looking educators including the highly renowned but not widely known professor Henry Mintzberg of McGill University agree that tenure should be eliminated. It now furthers what it was originally designed to avoid. I believe tenure at all levels should be abolished. Teachers should instead be measured on their value to students (it is already being done in some cases) and the top six nominated annually for the Nobel Prize. **Let's remove safety in teaching and replace it with reverence for teaching.**

The CEO of a major international company was selected to be Dean of the School of Business at one of America's better known universities. He was selected because of an eminently successful career of high level performance in a firm with over 100,00 employees. Because he was practical and looked for results rather than focus on theory he was not understood by the professors. The end result: a brilliant leader was unable to use proven and practical ideas to increase the faculty's value to students. There is a place for both theory and practical application. Exceptional leaders major in practical applications and minor in theory. Recommended reading: *The Witch Doctors* by John Micklethwait and Adrian Wooldridge.

Here's a thought worth keeping prominently displayed for you and your people to see daily:

"LIFELONG LEARNING IS THE GREAT EQUALIZER"

---

To act incessantly or redundantly. Make certain your goals are always relevant. Make all necessary changes

> *The way a leader handles failure reveals more*
> *about the leader than how the leader handles success*

Remember the example of Warren Gregory. He was not a "natural" leader. In his first attempt at the divisional manager's job he failed and stepped down to his prior job. He spent the next two years studying leadership and management and persuaded the company to give him a second chance at the divisional management position. The difference this time was that he understood the requirements of the job. His mastery of the job, on his second attempt, is a testament of his willingness to learn new skills and competencies. He had the right attitude and invested the time and energy needed to learn new skills. He could clearly distinguish between *having a failure* and *being a failure.*

By not branding himself a failure he was able to realize what it was he had to learn. Exceptional leaders learn from their failures and start all over again. *It is vital to recognize that having a failure does not make you a failure. Review your failures, see what there was for you to learn and then release them.* You can make your failures valuable by using them to avoid making the same mistakes again and move onward and upward.

**How Can You Be Sure You Know What You Have to Know?**

A motto for many could be *"I don't know that I don't know, therefore I think that I know!"*.

**Most people give themselves credit for knowing a lot more than they actually know.**
*A well-informed person today knows he doesn't have all the answers. . . and knows how to find them when necessary.* In this time of ever increasing change, with the ongoing need to learn and to remain informed, "on-line, off campus" electronic delivery of information is increasing exponentially. It may well become the way most people will prepare for entry into a business or profession. It is already a *vastly important* part of the learning necessary to stay current in many businesses and professions. America's corporations spend more on education than all of the colleges and universities. In many cases, the survival of a large number of colleges and universities will require that they integrate theory with practical, real-life training and become "partners in progress" with corporations. The governors of 14 western states joined forces and have created a "virtual on-line" accredited university. Phoenix University with a larger enrollment than either Stanford or Notre Dame, offers accredited degrees in a number of subjects on-line with no need to ever visit the campus. A new on-line high school, Cyber High in Ojai, CA has students enrolled from across the United States and a number of other countries. They have the largest campus in the world but no physical buildings. There will be many more such on-line schools. Traditional "schooling" as we know it will continue to undergo ever greater changes. **Education is the number one national security issue facing the US.**

**Only a well-informed person can make a well-informed decision.** *There is a shocking increase in executive level functional illiteracy.* Going on-line can help reduce it. Contrary to a lot of publicity, being on-line is not the answer to a leader's future . . . it is, however an ever more vital tool. With changes taking place all over the world, it is not possible to remain well informed without the personal use of on-line services. Being able to access the Internet/www enables a person to instantly search all over the world for facts, figures, studies, breakthroughs, challenges and changes that often have high impact on top level decisions. Without the ability to instantly search for required information, it is ever more difficult to make well-informed decisions. It is time for the personal computers found in top executive offices to be plugged in and used by the executive.

The Internet/www is likely more important than the discovery of the printing press. This critical function can no longer be *totally* handled by a staff member. Sometimes the use of the Internet/www is the most elegant and efficient way to distribute and receive information throughout your organization as well as throughout the world (Extranet). 1995 was the first year that (1) more e-mail (95 billion) was sent than US Postal mail (85 billion), (2) more PCs were purchased than TVs.

### There is no place on earth where information cannot reach.

A man told me about fourwheeling through the desert in the Middle East and seeing a group of men in several tents. He stopped to talk to them and discovered they were watching CNN on a portable uplink while sending and receiving documents on their cellular computer. There are already virtual companies in which key people live far away from each other and communicate via electronic methods (e-mail, videofax and telephone conferences). There will be many more.

**Information and Information Technology are _each_ to business what the neutron bomb is to warfare**. *No organization will survive without understanding how to use them.* There is more technology in the newest singing greeting cards than was aboard Apollo XI on its way to the moon. The new Nintendo game retailing for $250 has information technology that cost $14 million in the 1980s. In intelligent organizations the moment R&D starts a project it appears on the screens of engineering, finance, sales and marketing (as well as key clients). Everyone's input, right from the very beginning, helps shape and focus a product for its market. The same use of technology is already used in small businesses. For example, retailers can now sell custom-made bicycles, shoes, shirts, etc. using a direct computer link to manufacturers who will customize the item (s). Trying to lead an organization without access to on-line information would be the equivalent of a professional farmer plowing with a horse.

**You must know the vital difference between gathering information and business intelligence**.
*Become and remain well informed about every aspect of your industry, business, and your team members.* ***Organizations large and small _at all levels_ need superb business intelligence to survive***. Because of the Internet/www even small organizations can have better intelligence than the US and Russian governments had during the cold war. It was the Internet/www that prevented the coup against Gorbachev from succeeding. Herbert Meyer, author of *Real World Intelligence* warns, *"An organization traveling to the future without a thoughtful and precise intelligence program is as risky as the crew of a commercial jet liner flying in bad weather with the radar turned off."* For example, if your firm is in the wholesale fish business you should be aware of economic growth in China. Their rising standard of living will cause the price of certain fish to reach exorbitant levels and cause dramatic shortages. Recommended reading: *Competitive Intelligence* by Larry Kahaner.

### INTELLECTUAL CAPITAL GREATER THAN MONEY CAPITAL?

Walter Wriston, the visionary banker who built Citibank to be the largest US based bank by being a pioneer in the use of technology, claims that the basis for wealth has evolved from land to labor to information. He believes all revolutions are caused by a shift in power. He claims this is happening right now on a worldwide basis. Today, it seems intellectual capital is equal to or greater than money capital. The public stock market value of Microsoft is almost eighty billion dollars; the public stock market of General Motors is forty billion. Microsoft has no significant capital investment while General Motors has enormous amounts of required capital in its manufacturing facilities. Microsoft's ratio of book value to market value is one to twelve; General Motors ratio is one to one and a half.

# THE KEY DIMENSIONS
# OF
# LEADERSHIP

**THE KEY DIMENSIONS OF LEADERSHIP
LAY A FOUNDATION UPON WHICH YOU CAN
BUILD YOUR LEADERSHIP ABILITY.**

*The following sections detail each dimension.*

**VISION**

*"Imagination is more important than knowledge."*
*-Albert Einstein*

An integral part of exceptional leadership is vision. "Vision" is defined as the ability to bypass the obvious and see opportunities that evade others; to link the unlinkable; to change the structure of things--to create new ways of connecting things--to see new ways of doing things. It is a form of *futurethink*, looking at what is possible, unrestricted by extrapolating from the past. It enables the exceptional leader to see new and valuable relationships between many diverse ideas, events, things and people. Vision includes new discoveries as well as the rearrangement of long standing ideas.

**The force of a leader's convictions and scope of vision are often more vital than a position of power or authority.** It is strategically important for a leader to "put the cart before the horse" when defining objectives. *The end result must be identified before starting the process to achieve it.* Many people only extrapolate from the past and react to circumstances. To the contrary, exceptional leaders identify what they want to achieve first and then plan *back* to the present. Now, more than ever, it is critically important to have a sound vision before stepping into the future. The vision must be based on incorporating all available information on every aspect of your future goals but *must not* be restricted by that input. All industries and professions today are involved in the process of relentless change. The leaders who continuously expand their skill to understand and capitalize on change, rather than fight it or deny it, are the ones who will be successful. Remember, a common thread among most great leaders throughout history has been a devotion to lifelong learning.

---

**Here is an example of a lost opportunity:**

*In the recent past, the fax machine has changed the way letters and documents are transported and yet many firms that could have readily capitalized on this innovation failed to do so due to lack of vision.*

**Here is an example of seizing an opportunity:**
*French Telecom had a vision of capitalizing on the emerging market for numerous on-line services. Starting in 1980, they gave Minitel video terminals to access on-line services free to individuals and organizations they could then sell them the services. Today, there are more than twenty million Minitel users accessing more than twenty-five thousand different on-line services via the telephone.*

---

Vision is a competence that has been identified and associated with leadership for centuries. Exceptional leaders have a burning vision in their minds of how they want things to be, and do not allow the "day-to-day" to cloud their view. They keep the big picture in mind. They are obsessed with achieving their goals and allow nothing to stop them. Their vision is always stronger than any obstacles they may face.

*It is never enough to create a vision. It must be continuously revisioned.* Rarely is it the case when one individual single-handedly translates ideas into reality. What is required is drawing other people into the "vision" and rallying them behind it. The leader must be able to present ideas convincingly and generate enthusiasm in others. Helping people to participate in a "co-vision" that may seem a bit far out or beyond their imagination requires the ability to effectively communicate complex ideas in compelling, dramatic terms to create a *gestalt* so all can see, feel, and hear the "music." We are capable of far more than most of us realize. We honor people who run a 26 mile marathon. . .yet there are people in other parts of the world who run 70 to 100 miles non-stop on rough terrain and without fancy shoes.

Joe Batten, author of *Tough Minded Leadership*, emphasizes the need for vision, not only in top leaders but down through the management ranks. A production manager, to be consistently effective, must have a clear "picture" of how the organization should look and function now and in the future. The effective marketing executive must not only deal with current trends, but also must be able to "see," identify, and capitalize on future changes.

**The exceptional leader keeps one eye on the present and one eye on the future**. The future is not predetermined; it does not already exist. It exists only in our minds and in what we are able to conceive regarding how we want it to be. Financial services executive Frank Ciccarelli says, "*The best way to manage the future is to* attempt *to create it.*" Recognize the importance of "writing the last chapter first" and know that a clear understanding of where you are headed is necessary to carve out the most elegant path to that destination.

## THE FUTURE CANNOT BE PREDICTED; IT CAN BE PREPARED FOR.

"Visioning" is intuitive as well as intellectual. After vision is established, it must be continuously adjusted to capitalize on unforeseen changes. Much has been written on the right and left hemispheres of the brain. Current research indicates that intuition tends to be more of a right brain process, whereas the left brain is more concerned with the facts, figures, details and logic. The integration of both left and right brain is necessary for competent thinking.

> *When JFK announced in 1961 that the US would send a person to the moon and back safely, the media ridiculed him, and his own science advisors admonished him because no one had any idea how it would be done. His response was, "Now that the vision is in place, we will find the answers." The rest is history. Even if you are in a small organization and do not have major responsibilities, vision will aid you in creating and maintaining the "esprit de corps" necessary for long term success.*

Vision, however, comes from being able to better understand and capitalize on our intuitive right brain process. *You will most often get what you expect, not what you want. The secret then is to learn how to expect to reach whatever goals you set.*

Visioning, more than any other single factor, will help you to raise the expectations of yourself and all the people in your group. The deeper a clear vision is imbedded in the minds of all in the group the more likely it is to be realized.

The late science fiction writer Isaac Asimov (author of over 2,000 books) inspired many visions for high-tech companies. When he died, a number of them flew their flags at half mast as a tribute.

> *Inspired thinking will always be
> the highest form of technology.*

All of us are born with the capacity to conceptualize and think intuitively. It is a right brain function that begins to diminish by age 13 if not used and developed. As children most of us do use our ability to actively imagine but as adults we lose that ability, becoming encumbered in facts, details and data. The challenge is re-acquiring the ability to imagine.

**You can re-learn the ability to conceptualize at any age**. Take time to imagine, to daydream, to create new positive outcomes for all the challenges you face. Arianna Grace, author of the forthcoming book *Genius is a Light Sleeper* claims, "*Inspired thinking happens when the pathways between thought and flashes of genius merge. It is the magical union of logic and intuition. This level of awareness is available to all of us.*"

Do not confuse vision with strategies and goals. A vision is your ideal picture of the future. It is as if you were in a time machine catapulted 5, 10, 20 years ahead in time. If you could videotape everything that you saw, in great detail, and bring it back to the present, that would be your vision. Goals and strategies are then formed which become your road map for achieving your vision.

Extraordinary positive changes take place when people begin to use their ingenuity. **Futurethink,** by projecting three to five years into the future and defining the ultimate outcome your group would like to achieve. Act as if there were no obstacles to reaching your outcome. Then "back plan" a step at a time, to the present. This breaks the linear approach to thinking that blocks creativity. **Futurethinking** can be done by an individual or by an entire organization. Recommended reading: *The Holographic Universe,* by Michael Talbot.

**A leader's ability to reach a compelling vision will be challenged numerous times.** Leaders must convey strength when they feel weak, optimism and hope when things look hopeless. The strength of their convictions, their belief in themselves and their team members and the level of devotion to succeeding will likely determine the success or failure of the organization.
**Exceptional leaders remain strong in crises . . . and break down later when it's convenient.**

A crisis often unmasks a leader. During the darkest times in the early 1940s when the whole world was asking the question . . . "Can Britain survive?" . . . Churchill reframed the question by stating, *"Britain's goal is not to survive but to prevail."* A brilliant response by an exceptional leader.

**When the stakes are high, when the risks are great, when the outcome is in jeopardy, that's when you have to *earn the right* to be an exceptional leader.**

**VIP:** *Reflect for a moment* on how effectively you are using the opposite pages to record your thoughts, questions, insights and plans about how you will apply the material from this program.

# REVISIONING:
## A VISION MUST BE IN A CONSTANT STATE OF DYNAMIC CHANGE

The exceptional leader, as teacher and team builder, involves others in continuously revisioning and at the same time conveys a powerful viewpoint about the group: its destiny and how to reach it.

It is crucial that the vision of a group is continuously "revisioned." The group members must participate as co-visionaries. Exceptional Leaders involve their people and incorporate their ideas as part of the vision. Many leaders who begin as visionaries eventually begin to mistake their vision as a fixed destination rather than a perpetually renewing process.

**Many leaders have had to be replaced when their vision became rigid and inflexible.**

---

♦ *In 1903, a major scientific study determined that no machine heavier than air would ever fly. Later that year the Wright brothers, <u>after flying at Kitty Hawk</u>, were nevertheless convinced no airplane would ever be able to fly over the oceans. This was after they proved the study wrong.*

♦ *Einstein believed his work on atomic energy could not be used to develop a bomb.*

♦ *Thomas Watson, Sr., who originally built IBM into a powerful company (he was not the founder) did not want to switch from punch cards to electronic computers.*

---

## Every day is the first day of the future of your organization.

Your co-vision should include extrinsic and intrinsic goals. In addition to being better than your competitors, you need very clear and significant goals about what your group stands for, how it behaves and what it represents; its highest purpose. (See authentic organization discussion, page 30.)

*Exceptional leaders teach people <u>how</u> to think--not <u>what</u> to think*. It is not enough to outwork your past performance or your competition. You must also out-think yourself and your competitors.

When team members face obstacles, the exceptional leader <u>requires</u> them to find their best solutions to the obstacles before sharing the problem with the leader. Requiring people to create solutions causes them to reframe the way they see things. This causes them to function autonomously and be able to accept higher levels of responsibility and authority. Very often it reduces by 50% or more the time required by the leader to participate in creating solutions.

**A new twist on whistle blowing.** We furnish many of our clients with whistles for everyone in the group. We use the Fox 40, the most ingenious whistle in the world (see page 79). We ask each person to do several things with the whistle. 1) Keep it on their keychain as it may save their life in an emergency, 2) use it as a daily reminder of the need to be ingenious. 3) We encourage them to blow the whistle on anyone who is blocking progress including themselves. Imagine a meeting where all the attendees have a whistle and are encouraged to blow it anytime when anyone, including the leader of the group, is hindering progress. A number of our clients have found it to be an exceptionally effective tool, particularly in groups that are devoted to moving onward and upward. (It might not work well in a group where the leader is easily threatened.)

*No matter the size or length of success of an organization, the moment it stops revisioning its future, it starts to fail.* *Sears, IBM and Apple are examples of exceptionally successful organizations that stopped revisioning their future and suffered greatly.* Some organizations perish and others make successful comebacks by finally making the needed changes or bringing in new leaders who do. Sears and IBM brought in new decisive leaders. They changed the business philosophy to match the new vision. The market value of these two companies has increased over threefold. It remains to be seen what will happen to Apple.

**Only one of the top 100 US companies in 1900 is still in business. The other 99 no longer exist.**

Make **futurethinking** a regular part of your training sessions with both and large small groups. By focusing all your people's attention on the future they will be vastly more competent in dealing with the changes that they will be required to make (see the reference to Rene McPherson on page 24).

### *Women will have an ever more positive impact on all professions and businesses*

For years we have debated who is the father of modern management. The two names most often mentioned are Peter Drucker and Henry Mintzberg. However, it was recently discovered that in the 1920s a professor, M.P. Follett, wrote a book that includes many of the principles today's management and leadership books claim are required. Drucker found Follett's ideas to be so impressive he wrote the introduction to the republishing of Follett's book . . . Professor Follett's full name is Mary Parker Follett. The father of modern management was really the mother of modern management. Follett would likely be delighted to see the dramatic progress women have made.

To create a compelling vision requires the ability to integrate intuitive and logical thinking (integrated brain thinking). Women are much more skilled in integrated brain thinking than men. Additionally, a number of current studies show that women are excelling in all critical phases of leadership. They are proving to be more capable leaders than men. The percentage of women in executive VP and senior VP positions has doubled in the last decade. The current percentage will likely more than double in the next decade. The percentage of CEO positions for women may increase even more. The SBA estimates that women will own 50% of all US small businesses by the year 2000. Firms currently owned by women already employ more people than the Fortune 500 companies. The number of women securing patents has tripled in the last ten years. This is just the beginning. Within ten years it will make no difference whether a leader is a man or a woman.
**We will then finally focus on the appropriate issue - performance of the individual.**

A *10 year study of Fortune 500 CEOs showed that the higher the intuitive skill of the individual CEO, the higher the level of performance of the company over the long term. A direct relationship was proven between intuitive skill and corporate success.*

Forbes magazine's company of the year award for 1996 was won by Chrysler Corporation. Forbes cited their high levels of intuitive leadership as a major reason for their success.

# EXECUTION

### *Vision without action is simply hallucination.*
### *Action without vision is random activity.*

**A vision has to "make sense."** The exceptional leader is adept at translating vision into action. Having the ability to create a vision is not enough. The leader must work with others to build the strategies, develop the competence, discipline and judgment necessary to reach the organization's objectives. Additionally, if the leader is the CEO of the company, he or she must be able to identify and create the financial funding, the necessary structure and organization, and then carefully select the right people to successfully turn the vision into reality.

Some exceptional leaders who are not in top management end up being models for change by demonstrating consistently high levels of performance that "lead the way."

A major reason for continuous self-defeating procrastination by many, which can be easily overcome, is some combination of the fear of failure and/or the fear of success.[*] Both are powerful deterrents to taking intelligent risks. Never let anyone deprive you of the right to take risks. Investment banker Lou Witt states, *"Risk taking is not only a requirement, it is a privilege."*

There are many reasons for procrastination: fear, old habits, uncertainty, unrelenting resentment, entrenched interests, etc. Change is often seen as distasteful, painful, and requiring new skills.

Robert Kriegel, author of *If It Ain't Broke, BREAK IT*, and *Sacred Cows Make the Best Burgers* says, *"Exceptional leaders know that the biggest risk is not to risk. They are not afraid to make mistakes and encourage and reward subordinates for doing the same."* Responsible risk taking is a lot different from acting like a "loose cannon." Exceptional leaders get all the data, get input from all appropriate people, spend whatever time is necessary reflecting and only then make decisions.

### HOW TO BE YOUR OWN BEST EXPERT

**Exceptional leaders make their own decisions. They use others only as a source of possibilities.**

It is dangerous as well as unwise to allow so called "experts" to make your decisions. Especially the self ordained ones. A recent leadership book by a tenured professor is a good example. Among his many statements was a claim that while no business person had ever written a worthwhile book on leadership he qualified as an expert on the subject. His position is as absurd as a man claiming to be an expert on giving birth to a child while claiming that no woman could ever write a worthwhile book on the experience.

---

[*] See *How to Jump Start Your Brain,* by Christopher Hegarty.

Listen to others respectfully and require them to prove and defend their advice. For example, well informed patients are often likely to know more about the latest breakthroughs in medical treatments than even the specialists who treat them. Physician as "God" is a life threatening belief. The average life expectancy of a medical doctor in the United States is 58 years. They have proven that they do not have all the answers. Use an expert's input only when you are convinced it is sound. Irving David Shapiro, author of *You Must Not Let Them Con You! There's Too Much At Stake* has this to say about experts , *"For each and every expert, there is an equal and opposite expert."*
The O.J. Simpson trial has certainly proven that to be true.

Two elderly hoboes reminisced about their lack of success. One said, *"I went wrong by doing everything everybody told me to do."* The other hobo responded, *"That amazes me, I went wrong by never doing anything anybody told me."*

> *If you were building a major resort complex, it would be wise to plan the opening date first and then plan back from that so you know what you have to achieve as you make your way toward the final goal. For example, if you were building a complex over a five year period, and started from the opening date and planned backwards to the present, you would know exactly what date all the carpeting had to be through the loom at the factory to reach your project in time. (Late arrival of carpeting is one of the most frequent reasons for major real estate complexes not opening on time.) If it's not through the loom on time, you could take early steps to correct the problem. Operating back from your vision rather than waiting to get bad news will help prevent delays in opening on schedule.*

Once exceptional leaders (influenced by the input of others) have clearly established the ultimate "Co-Vision" for the organization, they work with and through all the people in the group to create a master plan that breaks down objectives into measurable tasks and clearly communicates them to every person in the group who must complete the work. Exceptional leaders in subordinate positions sometimes reach compelling goals without the aid and cooperation of top management.

## WHAT YOU SEIZE IS WHAT YOU GET

**There is nothing more common than talented yet unsuccessful people.** Many people can vision the future, but lack the discipline, drive and devotion necessary to capitalize on what they see. Without execution, all else is a waste of time.

**Execution turns the vision into reality.** Many good ideas have gone by the wayside because of an inability to translate "vision into action" and reluctance to take risks in executing. Exceptional leaders know that having the vision is only the start and that real success entails establishing the structure and having the irrevocable commitment necessary to do whatever it takes to succeed.

## SURVIVAL IS A MAJOR CONTRIBUTOR TO LONGEVITY

Many organizations have perished because their leaders refused to acknowledge that the organization required important, and in some cases, very dramatic changes to survive. They held onto doing things the way they had always been done in the face of irrefutable evidence that extraordinary changes had to be made. Only exceptional leaders have the capacity and the willingness to make major changes. Executive Robert Wooten states it this way, *"You must have a plan in place from which to deviate."*

# BE SURE YOUR ORGANIZATION SERVES YOUR BUSINESS
(Excerpted from "Leading Characteristics of Long Range Organizations." by Hegarty)

*Exceptional leaders see that the organization serves the business. In many companies the business is run to serve the organization. This is a major reason for failure and it is critical to know the difference. Businesses can no longer exist to serve the organization; the organization must make all necessary changes to serve the business.*

*Exceptional leaders "Maintain Humble Disrespect for the Status Quo." They see that tradition is respected . . . not revered. Rather than protect long standing policies, procedures and traditions that top management may prefer, organizations committed to survival and growth readily surrender tradition and make all necessary changes to increase the productivity of the business. Organizations that hold on to the past are commonly found among those who fail. (Organizations of any size, devoted to long-term success will make any and all changes required to remain competitive and profitable.) They attempt to continually beat themselves back to the market with new products even when they are already the leader.*

*One of our clients, a top performer in its industry for more than 30 years is at a moment of truth. It has excelled by building the highest quality, highest priced products in its field. However, its industry has now matured and industry growth is meager. Competitors selling modest quality products through national discount chains have now become the industry leaders. For the first time in the company's history it is losing money. It is facing wrenching changes that are necessary for survival. To remain in business, the company will have to build products of lower quality and drastically change its distribution methods. Will it be able to make all the changes necessary? Will it be capable of doing what has to be done to support the new business reality? Will outside leadership be required?*

*To survive, many corporations are finding it necessary to totally revise their corporate cultures. New strategies often required include: 1) continuous revisioning of their goals and objectives, 2) teamwork at all levels, 3) collaboration between management and labor, 4) giving the people doing the work the right to make decisions about how to do the work, 5) putting the customer first (not just claiming so).*

*What will you do if and when massive changes become necessary for the survival of your group? Think about it now. It is very likely to happen to your organization.*

*There are many examples of mediocre products and services historically that have been successful because of a superior disciplined business strategy. There are even more examples of superb products and services that failed because of the lack of a disciplined business strategy.*

---

*Today, the absence of a world class product or service guarantees failure--but the presence of a world class product or service does not guarantee success.*

*Two things are necessary--a world class product/service and a world class business strategy.*

---

# DECISION MAKING

**Difficulty in making decisions is an Achilles heel for many otherwise capable people.** It is most difficult for them in times of crises when life or death decisions have to be made quickly.

> *The ultimate power in decision making is to know that it is all right to change a decision as soon as you have evidence that it cannot work*

♦ *Exceptional leaders use exceptional judgment to avoid situations that may require exceptional skills. They develop exceptional judgment by not repeating the same mistakes. They find new ones to make and as a result develop exceptional judgment.*

**Exceptional leaders view indecisiveness as a _fatal weakness_ in subordinates.** It is a major reason for otherwise capable people to not be given more responsibility. A major factor in decision making is judgment. Sound judgment lies in the willingness to spend time intelligently analyzing data, getting input from others, reflecting and then making decisions.
**It is better to make a mediocre decision than no decision at all.**

*Exceptional leaders are more concerned with developing decision making skills in others than they are with making decisions themselves.* This enables them to achieve much more than they could if they continued to be involved in a large number of ongoing decisions.

*Teach your people to: Evaluate carefully; get sound input; reflect; make thoughtful decisions; monitor them relentlessly . . . and make changes when necessary.*

*Before executing your any plan, _masterfully organize_ _and prioritize the steps you will take_.* There are a variety of proven strategies that can help you reach your goals. Use practical, proven and potent strategies that others have used successfully. Recommended reading: *What America Does Right.* Author Robert Waterman identifies strategies that have made organizations successful for long periods of time.

No matter how small your organization may be, there are certain basic management systems you must master. 1) Basic financial controls: use of capital, cash flow management, exactly what profit each product makes, etc., 2) goal setting and relentless evaluation of progress, 3) clear, easy to understand job objectives and ways for each person to measure their own performance.

The reason many franchise businesses are successful while many independent businesses fail is the franchiser has operating manuals that clearly identify what must be done from A to Z and shows the franchisee exactly what steps to take every day. If you lack the basic management system skills, learn them before you start your own business.

Strategies for executing more effectively . . .

## Breaking The 80/20 Barrier

For a number of our client companies we have "profiled" the characteristics and skills of top performers in various functions. By hiring and training based on the profiles, clients have been able to raise the performance level of all the people in the group. For example, in a sales organization, where 80% of sales come from 20% of the sales force, the firm does not know how to maximize the performance of their sales force. A sales profile which identifies the actions, strategies, behaviors and attitudes of the top 20% is then used to develop the other 80%. (For example, optimists sell more than pessimists. . .yet most firms never test a sales candidate's level of optimism. In a study of agents for a large life insurance company it was discovered that optimists sold 37 times more insurance in their first two years than their pessimistic counterparts.) The end result: creating a profile and managing by it creates a dramatic increase in the performance of the entire sales force.

## Making Major Changes

To get the best results from a major change requires three crucial ingredients:

1. **A thorough understanding of how to make it work**

2. **An irrevocable commitment (sometimes it takes years to get the results)**

3. **Ongoing deep-level involvement by the top echelon of management**


Self-directed teams create dramatic increases in productivity while simultaneously increasing morale. RED FLAG: There have been disastrous results from self-directed teams when they were not carefully implemented. Many organizations lurch from idea to idea with no real commitment or understanding. Avoid *Flavor of the Month* management. Think out very carefully any changes you want to make.

**VIP:** *Reflect for a moment on how effectively you are using the opposite pages to record your thoughts, questions, insights and plans about how you will apply the material from this program.*

# TAKE TIME TO THINK

A requirement for successful execution of your plans is inspired ingenious thinking. Yet, over 70% of people in leadership/management roles "claim" to be too busy to think.

**Ingenious thinking at all levels of your organization is required if it is to survive.** Over 90% of business executives do not view themselves as highly competent thinkers. Yet there is no higher priority for leaders than learning how to think ingeniously. It is a skill that can be learned. There is little if any leverage in attempting to just out-work your own past performance. The real leverage is created by out-thinking your competitors and your own past performance. Leverage comes more from the brain than from brawn. **History shows that overcoming traditional ways of thinking is more important to a leader's success than a high IQ.**

## *Think in terms of solutions, not problems*

**Most people have never learned <u>how</u> to think. They have only learned <u>what</u> to think.** Jump start your brain--The greatest leverage available, in making the changes necessary to outperform your competitors and your own past performance is to teach ingenious thinking to all your people. Conduct thinking sessions. Create new ways of doing things--ask questions like, *"How can we do what can't be done?" " If we were to become (or to remain) the leader in our field, what would have to happen?"* Teach everyone to consider numerous alternatives to the way you do things. Get them to start thinking ingeniously. For example: hold a thinking session around the alternative uses of using two plastic bottles. Break your people into teams of two and have each team make a list of other uses for the bottles. Require each team to identify a minimum of 100 alternative uses. Encourage them to be outrageous . . . watch them start to develop their ingenuity. . . in a single session. **Continue to create opportunities for your group to be ingenious.**

I did a speaking assignment with Rene McPherson, the former CEO of Dana Corporation. During his 10 years as head of Dana, the productivity per employee (140,000 people in dozens of locations) more than doubled. I asked him "What was the single most valuable thing you did?" He answered "It was causing all the employees of Dana to join with a small number of others once a week. The subject was *What does the future hold? What role do I want to play? What do I need to learn?"* Dana then made training available to assist them. McPherson created the opportunity for all the employees of Dana to <u>join</u> <u>together</u> <u>in</u> <u>thinking</u> sessions. The outcome for both the company and the employees was one of the greatest success stories of American business.

**Exceptional leaders teach people to deal in solutions.** Most people think in terms of problems and have to be taught to create solutions. When you require your people to create solutions they use their ingenuity and perform at much higher levels of effectiveness. Do not accept a problem from a team member without a solution. Have each person identify his or her best solution and rate the solution from 0 - 10. They will rapidly begin to solve their own problems. This will reduce the amount of your time they need by up to 50%, while simultaneously improving their bottom line performance. People excel when they are in control and are required to find their own solutions. There are numerous proven examples of dramatic improvements in performance in both large and small groups when the individuals are given the responsibility and the authority for their job. Recommended reading: *Thinking in the Future Tense* by Jennifer James.

Often 80% of the challenge is in correctly identifying options and only 20% in executing the solution. Do *not* jump into action before thoroughly evaluating the challenge. Once this is done, then and only then, execute the plan ready to make any changes that might be required.

## LOOK FOR QUANTUM CHANGES

There is a vast difference between day-to-day execution and "Quantum Changes." Day-to-day tasks are the B priorities. Quantum Changes, on the other hand, focus on changes that can have a major, perhaps even life saving impact on the organization. These are the A priorities. Superb day to day execution is critical to the functioning of a group, but what creates continuous top performance is making Quantum Changes. There may be opportunities for you to create Quantum Changes right now. Look everywhere for them, you may find them right under your nose. For example, we have been able to show clients that offices are often a hindrance to high levels of performance.

*One of our client companies closed over 50 branch service/sales offices, which were replaced by vans equipped with all the latest cellular equipment. The company directed all service calls through a national 800 number. The result was 40% more service calls, a reduction of 4 million dollars in annual overhead, and a dramatic increase in customer satisfaction.*

Exceptional leaders teach people to identify the ultimate outcome by planning as if *nothing* were impossible. The leader asks such questions as, *"What can we do that has never been done? If time or money were not a problem, how could we accomplish the results?"* After examining all the options, the leader then works with team members to create an explicit plan to turn the vision into reality. Recommended reading: *Sacred Cows Make the Best Burgers* by Robert Kriegel.

**Exceptional leaders train themselves to see the tree and the forest at the same time.**

In *Reengineering the Corporation*, authors Michael Hammer and James Champy state that numerous organizations will perish unless they continuously find ways to "re-engineer" the way that they do business. They claim that re-engineering enabled:

1. A large company to increase its ability to service customer orders more than 100 times (not 100% but 100 times).

2. Another company improved its service to clients while reducing staff by 75%.

While there are no guarantees, exceptional leaders apply much thought about how to keep their employees and give them the opportunity to train for new jobs even if it will be with another firm. I did a seminar recently for the fastest growing division of a large telecommunications company. Rapidly changing conditions suddenly stopped their rate of growth and required that they rethink their strategy. The CEO of the division said to me the evening before the session, *"Chris, tell my people that they may or may not be here after the changes that are required. They should pay attention so they can use what they learn here or somewhere else."* He called me four weeks later to tell me that he had lost his job. In times of change often the most capable people are released. Never take setbacks personally. If you experience a setback see it as the first step to a comeback.

**Change or be changed. The choice is yours to make.** Whether it's called . . . "Quantum Changes," or "Re-engineering" or whatever, all organizations determined to succeed long term are required to continuously improve their bottom line performance. Remember . . . to change your organization . . . show your people why they should change. . . teach them how to search for Quantum Changes . . . and they will help change the organization.

*Opportunities for Quantum Changes likely exist at this moment.*
*It may require your organization to take new risks and/or change directions.*

Sometimes the opportunity for Quantum Changes are overlooked by very successful organizations. IBM was offered the opportunity to buy a struggling company called Haloid. Their market research indicated that there was a market for only 5 of the Haloid machines. Shortly after being turned down by IBM, Haloid changed it's name to Xerox. Years later Xerox manufactured the first personal computer (contrary to what most people believe, Apple was not the first) and abandoned it because they believed there was no market for it.

## DESTRUCTURING IS NOT ALWAYS DESTRUCTIVE

When an organization begins to destructure by changing traditions, revamping procedures, and downsizing its work group, many people see it as destructive.

This viewpoint causes them to be resistant to changing and limits their opportunity to seize the moment and make changes that would cause them to be more valuable to their organization or a new one they might join. Instead, they become commodities rather than valuable resources. A question we must all answer is whether *"to be or not be a commodity."*

**People who accept change and learn new skills develop a level of competence that will cause them to be seen as a vital resource to any organization looking for exceptional people.**

In 1900, over 20,000,000 people lived and worked on farms in the United States. Today, slightly more than a million do, and yet the United States is the breadbasket for the world. All those people who left the farm found other work. It will depend on your own level of competence and commitment what kind of work you will find.

An exceptional leader's credo could be expressed:

```
WE DO NOT OWE OUR PEOPLE A BRIGHTER FUTURE
WE DO OWE OUR FUTURE BRIGHTER PEOPLE
```

**Exceptional leaders continuously make their people brighter.**

# Vital Tasks Management

*Vital tasks management is a practical, potent and proven system for improving individual and group performance by allowing individuals to measure their own performance.*

**Vital tasks management gives individuals control over and responsibility for their jobs.**

Vital Tasks Management is something many managers think they're already doing. Many, however, are startled when they discover the discrepancies between how they think their subordinates view their jobs and how they actually view them. Whether hiring a new person or dealing with an experienced one, job performance will improve because of the clarity Vital Tasks creates.
**It is risky to assume how people view their jobs. . . discover how they actually view them.**
Vital Tasks will enable you to accurately determine how each person perceives his or her job.

There are seven key steps to Vital Tasks Management:

**Step 1:**
> The leader evaluates each person and position that reports to him/her and identifies the *specific measurable vital tasks* that are necessary for optimum performance. These are then broken down into clear, easy to measure tasks listed in understandable language.

**Step 2:**
> The leader has each individual look at his/her own job to identify their perception of the *specific measurable vital tasks* that would allow the person to optimally perform. These are also broken down into clear, easy to measure tasks listed in understandable language.

**Step 3:**
> **This is one of the two most crucial steps.** *The leader and team member merge these two lists through respectful empathetic negotiations. It is critical that negotiation be used, rather than the leader "dictating" the agenda to be followed.*

**Step 4:**
> The team member grades his/her own performance against the *specific measurable vital tasks* agenda on a regular basis and reviews this self-evaluation with the leader.

**Step 5:**
> **This is the other most crucial step.** *The leader reviews the self evaluation with each person individually on a frequent basis (weekly if possible). It's important to not focus on criticism or readily offer solutions in areas where the person is performing poorly. The leader solicits ideas from the team member on how he/she plans to correct the tasks that are being handled poorly. The role of the leader is to listen carefully and not impose solutions. This is a delicate and required step in building effective execution of Vital Tasks Management. Allow the person to solve the problem. Control, responsibility and ownership have now been placed in the team member's hands.*

**Remember, do not criticize or solve the person's problem.**

## Step 6:

The leader should solve a team member's problem only as a last resort. Each person is required to use ingenuity to improve the tasks where performance is poor. This allows each team member to experience control over, responsibility and ownership for his/her job.

*In most situations the people doing the work hold the solution to improving their job performance. Vital tasks management focuses their attention and interest on doing exactly that. The responsibility and authority of doing the job right is now clearly invested in the person doing the job.*

In many jobs people are put in a "pigeon hole," criticized when not doing the job right and punished for cooperating with or assisting other people. They lose interest in the job, begin to suffer from boredom, and eventually spend more time and energy getting out of work than would have been necessary to do the work. Because they feel that they don't count, and cannot communicate. They often quit the job mentally, and in many cases, quit the job in actuality. Vital Tasks Management helps prevent this.

**Vital tasks management creates higher levels of trust and rapport between leaders and team members.**

## Step 7:

The leader creates a vital task agenda for his/her own job and evaluates it on a regular basis.

**Why vital tasks management works:**

The major tenet of Vital Tasks management is that "most people most often live up to the level to which they are trusted--or down to the level to which they are distrusted. **People do their best when they are given the responsibility/authority for their own work and not harmed for admitting their weaknesses.** Operating against a vital tasks agenda causes people to be far more aware of what they're doing and increases their ability and interest in improving his job performance. Vital Tasks Management increases the productivity of individuals and groups by focusing on *results*.

Make sure that you do not mistake urgent issues as being vital. Most organizations have their best people solving problems rather than focusing on new opportunities. Assess carefully where your key people are focusing. If they are busy putting out fires, move them to capitalizing on your best and most profitable opportunities.

> **A good way to change behavior is to measure it . . . <u>the ultimate way to change behavior</u> is to allow individuals to measure their own behavior.**

# AN EXAMPLE OF VITAL TASKS MANAGEMENT AT WORK

excerpted from The Consistently Exceptional Salesperson by Christopher Hegarty

## "CATCH YOURSELF DOING IT RIGHT AND RE-INFORCE YOUR PERFORMANCE"

"Nothing happens until somebody sells something" is very misleading--when a salesperson is in a serious slump, many things are happening to the salesperson and they are harmful. Vital Tasks Management helps get through such crises with no permanent damage to the salesperson.

The best way to evaluate your performance as a salesperson is to identify the vital tasks that contribute to top sales performance and measure yourself against them relentlessly (one company experienced a 500 percent increase in first call sales by doing this).

*E.g.: The refusal/rejection dilemma and how to solve it. Over 65% of all sales calls end without the customer being asked to buy anything! This is because many sales people are unable to distinguish between refusal and rejection. They crave to be liked so much that they will fail at their work rather than risk feeling rejected. Evaluating your performance against number one will focus your attention on this crucial issue. While this is only one of three powerful steps to correct refusal/rejection, it alone can help dramatically.*

Use the following example of Vital Tasks Management as a starting point . . . study it and make whatever change is necessary to make it precise for your job.

_____1. I ask for specific action on every sales call, even if there is no chance for an immediate sale.

_____2. I listen to, not against, others.

_____3. I probe for a deeper understanding of each account on every sales call.

_____4. I delegate everything I can to everyone I can!

_____5. I teach people to treat me as a professional.

_____6. I call on the biggest prospects in my territory.

_____7. I call on the major decision maker at such prospects.

_____8. I use creative visual aids on every sales call.

_____9. I keep creative records on all accounts.

_____10. I organize my time for maximum efficiency and effectiveness.

_____11. I devote 2 hours per week to creative planning/evaluation.

_____12. I keep open communication with my manager.

_____13. I operate at ever higher levels of self-direction.

_____14. I operate from an ever deepening sense of calmness.

_____15. I evaluate my performance daily.

Evaluation: Identify what percentage of time you perform each task (e.g., if you call on the major decision maker one in four times, your score would be 25% of that particular task). Performing at 75% or more on each task will dramatically raise your effectiveness and results

## People excel when they are responsible for their own jobs.

---

Vital tasks management can be used for any job: this is an example of how a salesperson can use it with or without assistance from his/her boss.

***It is proven that work performance improves when people are in direct control of their work.*** One study divided a work group into two teams. Each team had to perform the same confusing and difficult tasks, while being continuously distracted by various sounds and noises in the background. One team was told to contend with the distractions the best that they could. The other team was given a control switch that they could push whenever they wished to stop the distractions. (The group with the switch was much more successful in performing the work . . . even though they never pushed the button.) Knowing they had the option gave them a sense of control over their environment. They were able to perform exceptionally well with only the knowledge that they were in control. This is just one example . . . a number of other such experiments had similar results.

Having worked as management consultants in a variety of organizations, both Phil Nelson and I have found that the most difficult step for most organizations to take is to fully grasp the requirement to train people to be responsible for their own jobs. Unless and until many organizations irrevocably commit to develop the confidence, autonomy and self-esteem of all the people in their organization, their very survival will be in ever increasing jeopardy.

***DON'T TRY TO HIDE THE OBVIOUS.*** *A challenge, threat or problem that people in a group perceive but is not openly talked about is more harmful than one that is openly discussed. . . .Only when an issue is clearly identified and openly discussed can all the individuals turn their attention to and use their ingenuity to solve the problem*

A major stumbling block for many leaders to capitalize on Vital Tasks Management is the leader's need to be needed. A leader with the need to be needed thrives on "putting out fires." A leader who excels at putting out fires is a " psychological pyromaniac." ˙

Exceptional leaders are _responsible to_ people (they select them carefully, train them thoroughly and do everything to assist their success). They do not accept _responsibility for_ their people. After doing everything possible to assist the person the exceptional leader will release the person if the person is not showing results. Many leaders keep people after they already know they will not succeed. They have become *responsible for* those individuals. The leader, the person and the organization are all harmed by this.

**It is better not to attempt major changes in an organization until top management is fully aware of all the requirements and is fully and irrevocably committed to making them.**

**VIP:** _Reflect for a moment_ *on how effectively you are using the opposite pages to record your thoughts, questions, insights and plans about how you will apply the material from this program.*

---

˙ See *Seven Neurotic Blocks to Leadership,* by Christopher Hegarty.

# INSPIRATION

*"Inspiration is highly contagious"*
*-Lou Witt*

Exceptional leaders are a positive and visible role model for others. They have learned how to inspire themselves and others to continuously perform at extraordinary levels for long periods of time. The vast majority of them are neither charismatic nor endowed with any special gifts or talents. They know exactly what they want to achieve and stay focused on it through good times and bad. Nothing deters them!

**They never allow their direct experiences to overpower their hope and vision for the future.**

All inspired leaders suffer from their own self-made magnificent obsession and are so resolute, so clear in their *values* (what they believe in) and their *value* (what they are capable of) that they cause others to follow them. People respond to exceptional leaders for several reasons: what they know, what they can and have accomplished, and perhaps most vital, who they are and what they stand for.

**You lead best by the example you set!** The capacity and willingness to change is a requirement for today's leaders. Your people are keenly sensitive about any discrepancy between what you say and what you do.

**It is not possible or necessary for you to be perfect. It is necessary for you not to act as if you were.** Your people will help where you're not strong--ask them for assistance. The more you try to conceal your weaknesses, the more magnified they will become in the eyes of your group.

## AUTHENTICITY

**Exceptional leaders are authentic leaders; they create a deep level of trust and rapport with people that is not otherwise possible.**

Food services executive Michael Hegarty states *"It is more vital who the leader is as a person than what authority the person holds. Today it is impossible to demand respect. It must be deserved."*

H. Ray Daley, Jr., of Wellspring Consulting, notes the need for a leader to be an authentic person. *"Authentic Presence is when what we think, say and do are the same. It enhances our ability to communicate successfully with others by being consistent, truthful, proactive and loving."* He identifies the ingredients necessary for developing an "Authentic Presence."

1. Call upon your courage in dealing with change.
2. Place your focus on the here and now.
3. Progressively refine your communication.
4. Seek to understand before seeking to be understood.
5. Respond rather than react.

Authenticity is outward expression of the exceptional leader's inner character. Communicate clearly your *values* (what you believe in, what you stand for) and your *value* (what you are competent at, what you are capable of) elegantly to all those who can impact your future. Recommended reading *Managing with the Wisdom of Love* by Dorothy Marcic.

Very often the authenticity of a leader is the reason others support the organization. Sometimes it is a life or death situation for the organization. Bankers and venture capitalists often make positive or negative decisions about funding an organization based on the authenticity of the principals. I was with a client at his bank while he was attempting to get a large loan necessary for the survival of his firm. The banker said *"Your financials do not warrant this loan . . . but I believe you do."*
He got the loan and built a successful firm. Another entrepreneur was turned down by 301 banks while attempting to finance his business. The 302nd banker believed in Walt Disney and agreed to finance Disneyland.

Sometimes the stakes are very high. The late Prime Minister Yitzhak Rabin of Israel was originally vehemently opposed to a peace plan proposed to him by former Israeli Foreign Minister Shimon Peres. However, after watching a video of Yassar Arafat expressing his desire for peace so authentically, Rabin reversed his stand and the outcome was that the three of them received the Nobel Peace Prize. It remains to be seen whether there will be peace in that part of the world. However, there is no doubt that the presentation made by Arafat was so genuine it caused someone who had been his bitter enemy to believe that peace was possible. Perhaps the reason Rabin could recognize Arafat's authentic plea for peace was because he succeeded as the leader of Israel by being totally authentic himself. Many people who disliked him and disagreed with him, voted for him because they knew they could trust that he would always do what he thought was best for Israel.

*Only authentic leaders have the possibility of reaching the hearts and spirits of others. They do this through credibility they have established with their people. It is only when this happens that ordinary people are capable of extraordinary accomplishments.*

> *People most often live up to the level to which they are trusted or down to the level to which they are distrusted.*

A 1996 survey done for Knight-Ridder claims that 83% of the American public believes that candidates for high level public office do not say what they mean or mean what they say. What a shocking indictment of the political tactics used to gain public office. What a magnificent opportunity for an authentic leader.

You can learn a great deal about a person by watching how he treats people who are not in a position to do anything for him.

To inspire people, make work *meaningful* for them; this is possible even in jobs considered boring! Most people want to be inspired . . . to find meaning and purpose in what they do.

In a study at Harvard University, Dr. David McClelland used a series of experiments designed to enhance the immune response of volunteer groups. The groups were made up of individuals with a variety of religious beliefs (including atheists), education, ethnic backgrounds, ages, interests, etc. One of the experiences caused the highest response in every group tested. It was a film about the life's work of Mother Teresa. **People are inspired by powerful, positive, meaningful experiences.** It is most often not classic charisma that makes a leader inspirational, nor is it physical stature, glibness or education. It emanates from the leader's passionate commitment, authenticity, having a vision and the drive to achieve it, communication skills, giving people control over their work and developing everyone to be a leader whether or not in management.

**Always be mindful that only authentic leaders can capture the hearts and spirits of others.**

**The Authentic Organization: It is the intrinsic goals that determine the authenticity of an organization.**

The authentic leader sets the stage for the authentic organization. Study carefully the mission statement and values statement of an organization. Evaluate whether it operates by them and you will have superb insight into the organization's authenticity or lack of it.

---

### EXTRINSIC AND INTRINSIC GOALS
(Excerpted from "Leading Characteristics of Long Range Organizations," by Hegarty):

*Long range organizations have clearly defined, clearly understood long-range objectives that include both extrinsic and intrinsic goals. The objectives are both demanding and understood by all to be important. Long range success seems to require more than just extrinsic goals (that is, such things as market share, product dominance, return on investment, return to share holders, etc.).*

*It is also equally important for organizations that want to succeed for a very long time to have clearly defined intrinsic goals such as: What do we stand for? Do we deliver value? Do we operate with honesty and integrity? What are the consequences for people working for us?*

*One of our client organizations, Black and Veatch, a world wide engineering consulting firm has remained at the top of its field for almost 80 years. Here is an excerpt from their mission statement:*

*Our goal will be to provide:*

- *Challenging work in a stimulating and professional environment.*
- *Opportunities for growth and professional development.*
- *We will accomplish our goals by re-affirmation of faith in our founding principles: honesty, integrity and dedication in dealing with clients, ourselves and others.*
- *As a diversified firm, we will operate with a common purpose, organizational unity, effective communication and competitive spirit.*
- *Remuneration and recognition consistent with performance.*

**Honesty and integrity are proven organizational longevity factors, but are not in vogue . . . are not even considered in many organizations . . . yet they are the soul and spirit of any group.**

Many organizations that succeed over long periods of time are devoted to the interests of all their stakeholders;
. . . customers, owners, stockholders and employees.

Businesses are not charitable organizations. They need not have a high moral purpose. They are required to accept full responsibility for the consequences of their actions.

Most people respond to leaders who are ethical, fully focused on what they want to achieve, clear about their *value* (what they are capable of) and their *values* (what they believe in) and who demonstrate both of them to others.

Exceptional Leaders are not always highly articulate public speakers and they may not always appear overly enthusiastic, but they have a deep passion to turn their vision into reality, which generates excitement in others.

**You can <u>develop</u> the skills to know *how* to convey a vision. To convey it correctly is as critical as the vision itself.**

It is a requirement for most leaders to be able to speak skillfully before a variety of groups. Yet, a survey of company CEOs showed that only 6% of them considered themselves competent public speakers.

Many leaders are perceived negatively by their people, such as condescending, distant, aloof, unreal, disconnected, etc.

> *When the leaders of Ford Motor Company determined to turn the company around in the early 1980s, the vision was to identify "the characteristics that would enable us to build a superb car buyers would value." People in every department; finance, design, marketing, engineering, R&D, both union and non-union workers, were inspired to do what they could to help determine the ultimate car that might be built. Ford Motor Company's turnaround is one of the greatest successes of the late twentieth century in American industry. An exceptional vision was inspired and executed with drive and empathy and propelled Ford to the top of the industry. More than ten years later, they are still reaping the rewards of the Ford Taurus. Their biggest challenge will be to continuously re-vision their future again and again.*

These leaders seem to communicate from behind a psychological prophylactic. This can be changed quickly if the leader wants to improve and has the right training.

**Eloquence is not necessary.** Nor is classical charisma. It is true that there are a few people (less than 1%) with the rare ability to inspire others in a matter of minutes. It is also true that many leaders have been capable of inspiring many people for long periods of time without any special talents or gifts. Charisma by itself is never sufficient for long-term results; there are many other requirements to be a long term inspirational leader. It is no longer enough to just talk the talk. **A leader today has to walk the walk and show others how to do it.**

Exceptional leaders continuously improve their communication. The ability to inspire others is often thought of as something people are born with, but many who would be considered introverts, have acquired the skills to inspire and motivate large groups. Quiet charisma emanates from a person who is "magnificently obsessed" to achieve a compelling vision and reaches out to include others in it. A vital factor in inspiration is integrity. It allows a leader to be consistent with his internal values and consistent in inspiring others. Be authentic--be real. It is only then that you will have the chance of capturing the heart and spirit of your people.

There is no valid reason a person cannot become a competent public speaker. The Institute offers breakthrough training in Public Speaking that can quickly improve a person's speaking ability. The *fear* of public speaking can be eliminated over the phone. (To learn how you can do this, contact Adrienne Fowlie of the Institute for Exceptional Performance at 415/892-0202.)

All speakers go through three stages of development: 1) Their attention is *on* themselves . . . unsure of how they are doing, 2) Their attention is *on* their material . . . comfortable with themselves they now focus on what they are saying, 3) Their attention is *on* their audience . . . comfortable with themselves and their material they now can pay attention to the audience. When speakers reach stage three they can begin to create high levels of rapport with the audience. With your attention off yourself and your material you can then learn to be *outrageously yourself* in front of an audience which is the secret of effective speaking.

Do not be held back by fear or lack of skill. Many leaders are reluctant to openly communicate their thoughts, feelings and dreams for fear they will look silly. Exceptional leaders are always willing to risk letting their mind show in public. It is a major factor in a leader's success to constantly develop better ways of communicating with all those necessary to carry out the vision. Keep refining and improving. Recommended reading *You Must Be Believed To Be Heard* by Bert Decker.

Inspiration begins with full disclosure. Tell the truth. As you reveal your thoughts, hopes, etc., others in the group will do the same. You will create clarity, cooperation and commitment between your people. You are *painting a picture* for others. Let them know what you're thinking. **A most common and costly mistake in communication is assuming too much. What is obvious to you may not be obvious to others.** Create the canvas, filling in the facets, corners and colors and lines. With some people, just a piece of the picture is enough and with others you *have to finish the whole picture*. Some people can virtually fill a blank canvas themselves, others can only paint by the numbers.

You can learn to be an ever better communicator: develop listening skills, questioning skills and the other skills to increase rapport with people. Take training in public speaking. Watch films of great communicators--Winston Churchill, John Kennedy and Martin Luther King are three examples. Many great communicators were ineffective before they worked to perfect their skills.

*While Churchill came to be known as a master communicator, he was totally inept at it until an otherwise unheralded American politician inspired him and taught him how to communicate. Without this role model, it is likely no one would recognize the name Winston Churchill.*

Take action. Make your ideas known. Use rich compelling language, great examples, metaphors, etc. Even more vital: be authentic; show who you are; practice with video; join Toastmasters. Recommended reading: *Leading Out Loud*, by Terry Pearce.

# THE FUTURE BELONGS TO THE OMNICOMPETENT

*"The mightiest of all warriors is he who can conquer himself."*
*-Confucius*

## WHAT IS OMNICOMPETENCE AND WHY IS IT NECESSARY?

**Omnicompetence** in an individual is made up of strong **basic intelligence,** high levels of **emotional intelligence** (which is made up of more than a half dozen areas), and **intuitive intelligence** (which contrary to common belief can be learned at any time in a person's life).

However, it is not enough to be skilled in each of the three above areas but it is also necessary for a person to live in a state of awareness that allows the person to access and integrate each of them. Reflect for a moment on someone that under normal circumstances exhibits high levels of basic intelligence coupled with emotional intelligence and sound intuitive judgment. What happens when he or she is under relentless stress and continuous change? That is the real test of whether the person is **omnicompetent** and suited for the challenging evermore complex world in which we live. Training is now available to enable an individual to develop the three levels of intelligence and the necessary skills to function under unyielding pressure during times of crisis.

*"To stay ahead of those who think they are out in front"* is required to achieve long term success. Today all organizations have to perform at ever increasing levels of competence with less time, money and resources. Those without people of strong basic intelligence, highly developed emotional intelligence, and equally powerful intuitive intelligence will be "hurtling" through an ever changing world unaware of whether an obstruction lies ahead or not. **Omnicompetence** allows a person to see around corners.

## REMAINING INSPIRED

**The most critical factor is for the leader to remain inspired.** Self-inspiration is a requirement for long term success and it can be enhanced by a high level of self-understanding. Consider the wisdom of this statement:

> *Seek to understand the Universe and you will understand nothing.*
> *Seek to understand yourself and you will understand the Universe.*

**Emotional Illiteracy: A Major Cause Of Failure.** Are you emotionally illiterate? Peter Drucker says *"Self understanding is always the toughest area for executives to focus on."*
Your IQ is only one factor in achieving success as a leader. Another is your <u>emotional intelligence</u> . Some researchers believe the majority of the factors (80+ %) necessary to succeed long term as a leader are based on *emotional intelligence*. Many people resist looking inward. **They are emotionally illiterate and have become fugitives from themselves**. This area is no longer an option, it is required learning to be an effective leader. Most people never ask themselves why they behave the way they do. More people know their astrological birth sign than the location and function of their spleen. The more you know about yourself, the better equipped you will be to organize and execute a self directed plan to achieve what you want both personally/professionally. It is possible to evaluate your talents, identify and change introjected values, and make many other changes that will improve your leadership.

Here are six of the basic emotional intelligence skills. Evaluate yourself 0 - 10 as you are now.

1) **self awareness**...the ability to identify your feelings, reactions and habits
2) **management of your feelings**...controlling your own moods and impulses
3) **self motivation**...maintaining persistence, optimism and drive
4) **empathy**...the ability to identify and respond to what another person is thinking or feeling
5) **people skills**...interacting successfully with others.
6) **ego mastery**...developing an evolved ego.

While many leaders refuse or are unable to see their weaknesses, people around them see them clearly. In some ways they know more about the leader than the leader does. Recommended reading: *Executive EQ* by Robert Cooper and Ayman Sawaf.

**There is yet another intelligence necessary to be omnicompetent - intuitive intelligence.** Most people believe that a person is either intuitive or not. The truth is intuition is a skill that can be learned at any time in a person's life just like riding a bike or operating a computer.

Many leaders find lasting value in reading about others who have overcome great obstacles. Recommended reading, *Man's Search for Meaning* by the late Viktor Frankl. A Viennese psychiatrist and author, he lost most of his family during the Second World War to the Nazis and spent years himself in concentration camps. Yet in that most tragic environment he found a reason to survive. . . to help others survive. After the Second World War he made a new life, started a new family and devoted his life's work to helping people understand what he learned in the concentration camps. His school of psychology, Logotherapy, has helped numerous people survive great losses and begin again. His courage and willingness to accept what he could not change has been an inspiration to millions. I met Frankl in 1975 and spent a long time talking with him. He was then in his 70s and exhibited extraordinary high levels of optimism and hope. He survived the greatest losses possible and yet still found value and worth in living. He lived to be 92 years old. While I learned much from him, the one statement that has always remained clearly in my mind is: *"A person can survive any loss, accept any circumstances if he has a vital enough reason to live."*

**Create a gallery of your heroes.** Surround yourself with pictures of men and women who inspire you (attach to each picture the statement(s) that mean the most to you). During moments of great challenge, it will give you added strength and inspiration. Many of our seminar attendees have said this helped them get through their biggest challenges by enabling them to call on their deepest reservoirs of courage and determination. I have been lifted through a number of devastating losses by using my gallery for support. In remembering what I learned from each of them I was able to see past the moment of trial.

**Be bold . . . confident and humble . . . consider including prayer in your daily priorities.** Many leaders find inspiration in the scriptures relative to their faith. Prayer is a proven leadership tool. Double-blind studies, by major universities and other groups, have scientifically verified that prayer produces measurable results. I have met a large number of leaders who credit their success to prayer. Recommended reading: *Healing Words,* by Larry Dossey, MD

To inspire others, remember

## WE DO NOT OWE OUR PEOPLE A BRIGHTER FUTURE.
## WE DO OWE OUR FUTURE TO BRIGHTER PEOPLE.

# DRIVE

*"The force of an exceptional leader's drive is greater than the force of gravity."*
*-Ilonka Harezi*

Drive is the intense desire to succeed and not allow obstacles to deter one's actions. Exceptional leaders have high levels of drive, "obsessed" with accomplishing a vision. Clarity of direction enables them to eliminate "obscurely relevant" distractions while moving directly toward the goals. There are two distinct forms of drive. One is a magnificent obsession with accomplishing demanding objectives. The other has a negative origin emanating from low self-esteem causing someone to be driven to avoid failure. It is often seen in "workaholic" behavior. The two kinds of drive may be very similar in impetus but are very different in consequences to the leader.

***Drive is what makes leaders forceful and propels them to meet their goals.*** For many exceptional leaders the *primary* drive is often not to personally achieve or affiliate but to organize and execute plans that cause others to achieve and affiliate. They see themselves as responsible for organizing, communicating with and joining with others to get the job done.

> *Exceptional leaders may or may not <u>stand out</u> in a crowd, but are willing to <u>stand apart</u> from any person or crowd that will hinder them from what they are trying to achieve.*

Exceptional leaders are very clear about what they want to achieve and invest no time in people, events or activities that do not contribute to the goals they have established. They are willing to risk being disliked and/or misunderstood whenever it is required to get the job done.

*Exceptional leaders never <u>pursue</u> being popular although it may <u>ensue.</u>* They are totally devoted to reaching their goals and while they may be demanding and tough, they are also often fair.

*They focus on the successful outcome--and lack the "common sense" to know when to quit.* They see problems that would cause others to give up as challenges to overcome.
They know that ***commitment is not how long or how hard you work. . .it is a line you cross.***

History has shown the importance of drive in the success of a leader. There is story upon story of individuals who had ideas turned down but who kept coming back until they succeeded. A person's drive is not always a desire for monetary success but is often a passionate commitment to accomplish something significant--a deep continuous striving to fulfill one's potential. The leader with high levels of drive doesn't give up but continues to change strategies until finding the way to attain the goals and objectives set for the organization. Exceptional leaders dramatically increase the drive of others through example. Involving your people as co-visionaries creates a high level of commitment from all members of the group. You are more likely to accomplish something significant if it is seen as valuable to *all* the people involved.

Drive, however, may not always have a positive origin. It may sometimes come from lack of self-esteem. Many people are driven to be successful because of underlying feelings of inadequacy. While this is a major contributing factor in many success stories, it is much more exciting and enjoyable to be drawn to succeed from a passion to participate in something that is important and valuable to you and other people. There is a great difference between "working hard" (positive drive) and "workaholism" (negative drive).

Some leaders are striving to achieve because of a sense of joy and passion. The workaholic leader is driven by a high state of anxiety. Accomplishing something is necessary for that person to avoid a sense of failure. Tom Watson, Jr., said his motivation to succeed as CEO of IBM was an acute fear of failure. He was fearful of not being the right successor to his father, Tom Watson, Sr. While a person of high self-esteem is participating in a passion for achievement and finds joy in the process as well as in the achievement, the low self esteem leader is rarely able to savor his accomplishments.

Drive is the force that propels people to succeed. We can also look at it as what we *want to acquire* as well as what we *want to become*. The drive to acquire is what we experience when we want to gain something tangible. Our drive to acquire often depends on many factors such as our social and professional standing, our current level of satisfaction with our material success, with our lifestyle, home, automobile, ability to travel, etc. The day comes for many when this drive may diminish.

Many people in leadership positions have no compelling agenda of what they want to achieve. *They often want the position more to complete their resume rather than for the challenges and opportunities it presents.*

**The drive for what we most want *to become* emanates from within.** It is the desire for significant achievement that "draws" individuals forward and upward. Use the model that has worked for long-term leadership success. *Compelling extrinsic and intrinsic goals. . . Purposeful service to others . . . honesty. . . morality . . . integrity . . . authenticity.*

Your drive is shaped by the difference between the vision you hold in your mind of how things could be and how they actually are. For example, if you are an entrepreneur, you may have a clear vision of wanting to create a major success and yet have not been able to do so. As you cling to the vision and the reality has not yet occurred. this causes a "dissonant state". This, in turn, creates a high level of drive to alter your reality and make it fall into line with your vision. Try new ingenious approaches until you reach your goal. Match your vision with action. Remember our discussion about vision:

*Vision without action is hallucination.*
*Action without vision is random activity.*

---

See *Making a Living While Making a Life . . Hard Work is not Workaholism,* by Christopher Hegarty.

For many individuals who score low on the drive scale, the cause is a lack of vision. They have not clearly identified what is important to them and what they would like to do. Unless and until they develop the skill of _vividly visioning_ a bright future, they are unlikely to ever achieve much.

Highly recommended reading: _The Act of Will,_ by Roberto Assagioli; begin with chapter 5, _The Skillful Will: The Psychological Laws_, then read the entire book. Many people have gone from failure and frustration to success by using Assagioli's uniquely valuable principles.

**Have you discovered what you would most value doing?**

Drive is not a static condition. You can increase your drive and the drive of others by being involved in achieving an outcome that you and they _choose and value highly._ Your values will help you identify the right situation. For example, if you have high social values, and also want to earn substantial money, you would do much better in a situation where you could be of valuable service to others as well as make a lot of money rather than in a situation where only power and/or money can be achieved. Your innate natural drive is released when you work toward truly fulfilling goals you are passionately committed to achieving.

You may score low on the drive scale because of no life focus or clear goals. You may have ended up in an occupation or career that provides little if any satisfaction. Many people have left one occupation for another in order to find purposeful exciting work--the mediocre corporate executive, for example, who quits and becomes a successful, contented chef and restaurateur. Mother Teresa was in her forties before she discovered her life's work of helping the poor.

## DO WHAT YOU VALUE--DO WHAT EXCITES YOU!
_Talents and Skills:  What is the difference?_

### You can't change the world . . . but you can change _your_ world.

Studies claim that 80% of all people are in jobs not suited for them. No wonder research indicates that fewer than 5% of individuals know their inborn talents. Yet knowing your talents, as opposed to your skills, is crucial to finding appropriate work. (The Institute offers assistance in helping individuals uncover their talents.) Make a list of all the opportunities that you value. Look at these against a variety of occupations and careers, including your current one. Often a person will feel trapped and reluctant to consider a change but upon further examination will realize that most of these "traps" are in his or her own mind. There are many forms of work you can learn to do successfully.

Exceptional Leaders are not always primarily motivated by material gain, power or personal fame, but are often drawn by a passionate desire for specific achievements that they value highly. When this is the case, it is not a struggle for success, but a joyful and challenging odyssey. The key to biological survival is the ability to adapt to the occupied niche. The same can be said of work. _How well do you fit your job niche?  Or perhaps it is better to ask, how well does your job fit you?  Are you miscast in your work role?_

**You can make the grass greener on your side of the fence.**

However, it is also true that finding happiness and contentment in your work, as well as in life, is based more on your view of them rather than the situation itself. You may well *choose* to enjoy your current job rather than seek new employment. Rethink why you do what you do and you may discover how to create a way to like and value your current work.

Many people have mistakenly "learned" to not enjoy their work. In reality, to miss experiencing the joy of your labor is one of the greatest personal losses a person can suffer. Your long-term health and your life expectancy are both intimately affected by how you experience your work.

Many people spend more time and energy getting out of work than it would take to do the work. Everybody loses when someone does not do their job the best they're capable of, but no one loses as much as the person who doesn't savor the joy of his labor.

> *That is not to say that every job is worth keeping or that a person should not seek a job in line with her values, talents and interests.*

It is very easy to see the difference in a person who joyfully works and one who doesn't.
 **A person who works with joy radiates a spirit of delight in what he is doing.** The person who works with distaste is disinterested. dispirited, and often sullen.

My friend and teacher, Vincent Stroops, lived to be 101 and died a young person. He lived by five principles of wisdom. His principle regarding work was *"I experienced the joy of my labor everyday I went to work, no matter the job, the conditions, or the boss. I devoted myself totally to doing the finest work I was capable of everyday. My attitude about my work was self chosen and was not influenced by any other person or conditions."*

Another one of his five principles was *"Never meet anyone important enough to hate".*
He explained *" I discovered as a young person that to hate someone destroys the hater.*
*I promised myself I would never meet anybody who could be that important. Rather than resent someone or want to get even , I focused all my attention on doing my job better.."*
*"Don't get even...Get ahead"* is far better than the old maxim *"Don't get mad....Get even!"*

I have seen change in individuals who altered their viewpoint about work from negative to positive. It is as if they have become different people even though they are doing the same job.
Experience the joy of your labor daily. No matter the job . . the conditions . . or the boss!

> When all is said and done, have you done more than you've said?

*Work is love made visible ... and what is it to work with love? It is to build the sandals as if your beloved were to wear them. It is to crush the grapes as if your beloved were to drink the wine ... ... **it is to charge all things you fashion with a breath of your own spirit.***
>                                    Kahlil Gibran


**Experience the joy of your labor daily. No matter the job...the conditions...or the boss!**

## OWNERSHIP

*"The buck stops here"*
*-Harry Truman*

Exceptional leaders have a high level of personal "ownership." This is the level of accountability that exists for oneself and one's actions. They accept personal responsibility for both successes and failures, realizing that experiencing failure does not make one a failure. They easily regroup after setbacks, learning from them and creating new and ingenious strategies to reach their vision and do not blame anybody or anything. Exceptional leaders never take setbacks personally and can easily distinguish between having a failure and becoming a failure.

*Until one is committed, there is hesitancy, the chance to draw back, concerning all acts of initiative (and creation). There is one elementary truth the ignorance of which kills countless ideas and splendid plans: That the moment one definitely commits oneself, then providence moves too. All sorts of things occur to help one that would never otherwise have occurred. A whole stream of events issues from the decision, raising in one's favor all manner of unforeseen incidents and meetings and material assistance which no man could have dreamed would have come his way. Whatever you can do or dream you can, begin it. Boldness has genius, power and magic in it. Begin it now.*

*-Goethe*

Exceptional leaders approach work, and life in general, with a strategy that can be identified as 100/100 responsibility and teach others the same approach. They accept that they are always, without exception, totally responsible for the output of the group. If every person in the organization accepts the same 100/100 responsibility (*full* acceptance of responsibility for the output of the group) most people will eagerly participate in the ownership and execution of the organization's goals. When people in a group take less responsibility, the measure of how much accountability each individual is accepting is open to subjective measurement. Responsibility is not a two way street. When all the individuals are willing to do everything to get the job done, there is total cooperation and commitment.

**In a 100/100 group:**

- ◆ **THE PRIMARY FUNCTION OF EACH PERSON IS TO BE AS VALUABLE AS POSSIBLE TO THE PEOPLE THE GROUP SERVES**

- ◆ **THE SECONDARY FUNCTION OF EACH PERSON IS TO DO THE SPECIFIC MEASURABLE JOB HE OR SHE IS PAID TO DO**

There are two categories that clarify the concept of personal accountability: "externals" and "internals." Externals are people who believe that the direction much of their life takes is really out of their control.They feel they are victims of fate and circumstance, products of destiny.Their career success depends more on what company they happen to land in and what type of boss they happen to draw.

They are quick to pass blame. That blame may be directed toward parents who weren't intelligent and didn't provide enough direction or foster enough independence or may be directed toward their experience or lack of experience. *"If I'd just gone to the right school or had the right breaks"* are common statements of externals. Often blame is directed toward co-workers. An external production manager blames failures in the production department on poor research and development. Salespeople who are externals may blame manufacturing for poor quality products and, in turn, slacking sales. Externals create an illusion of blamelessness for themselves. They are deceiving themselves, wanting to believe they are not responsible for their poor performance. In time of reversal and loss they perceive themselves as helpless victims rather than accept the responsibility to get up and get going!

Exceptional leaders on the other hand, are internals. They look inside themselves for solutions to problems and know if an answer is to be found they will find it. They know they will likely determine whether or not a project is to succeed or fail. It is "total ownership," a remarkable sense of personal accountability that enables them to cut through many of the obstacles that others might see as impossible to surmount. They know there *is* a way to solve the problems and, even though they might not currently see the way, persist until they find it! The pathway to exceptional leadership requires an acceptance of ultimate responsibility. The leader's value is determined, to a large degree, by belief in oneself and in others to develop the competence and confidence necessary to achieve the vision. Any obstacle or setback is seen as an inconvenience and does not deter the exceptional leader from moving forward.

RED FLAG. **Most programs on participative management and empowerment have failed.** A major reason is that they do not clearly convey the reality of responsibility to each of the individuals. Many people mistakenly perceive empowerment to mean taking power from someone to give to someone else.

> *Lifetime job security? Not in this lifetime!*
> *The only job security that exists today is continually increasing*
> *your competence and performance.*

**The career ladder has been changed to a tightrope.** The days of joining an organization where *"you had to know someone to get fired"* are gone. Even in organizations like public utilities, fire districts, government agencies and large well-established firms, jobs are at much greater risk than in the past. The US Supreme Court--long immune to performance reviews--is undergoing its first fiscal audit ever by the General Accounting Office of the US government. *Continue to be ever more valuable--develop new skills, expand your flexibility--you will always succeed . . . somewhere.*

A vital ingredient of accepting ownership is that exceptional leaders know a person is more than the total of his/her wins and losses. These are things that happen to you; they are *not* what you are. A way to state this might be, *"I will give my very best to make this work. I will enjoy the win or be disappointed by the loss, but in no way will that brand me capable or incapable."* Exceptional leaders do not take the outcome of their activities personally. They *own* them but if something goes wrong, for whatever reason, they are able to recoup quickly and begin again.
**They have learned to fall up the stairs.** People who take failure personally are unlikely to venture out and try again. They mistake *having* a failure with *making them* a failure!

Winston Churchill was once asked to explain why he continued to try after having had so many failures throughout most of his life. He replied *"I determined early in life that if I wanted to make something of myself I would have to <u>go from failure to failure enthusiastically</u> until I finally succeeded*

**Strange as the idea may seem at first, humility'** **is an important leadership strength.**
 It was humility, perhaps more than any other single factor, that allowed IBM to create the computer industry (it did not create the computer) and reign supreme for more than three decades. IBM was willing to make any changes necessary to remain the leading innovator in their industry. However, somewhere along the way IBM stopped revisioning their future and ran into major difficulties. Exceptional leaders admit openly they are not perfect . . . and then organize their group to call on the leader's strengths and find others to excel where the leader is not strong. They involve the entire group in the responsibility for the organization's success. They have clearly defined objectives that they are always willing to change if and when necessary. It is humility that allows them to change without embarrassment or self ridicule.

**Focus on the impact you can have on the future.**
**Do not focus on the impact the future may have on you.**

*A key strategy in developing ownership is the process of goal setting. Develop a sense of ownership in yourself and others by setting goals and executing a plan to achieve them.* A good way to start is by listing all the goals you would like to achieve, not being bound by whether you think it is possible to reach them. Then prioritize them and categorize them. If interested in making your personal life successful as well as your business life, establish integrated goals in both areas. It is possible to maintain a good balance between the two. Once you've established and prioritized your goals, go back and review carefully how you're going to achieve them. Having a goal that you are irrevocably committed to achieving is the most important ingredient.
*Again, be certain you understand the difference between persistence and perseveration.*

If you scored lower on the "ownership" scale and have not been goal oriented, start now with goals that are attainable. It's much better to set modest goals and achieve them rather than setting goals that you believe are out of your grasp. Achievers set goals that are possible, and expand them rapidly as they are met. Clearly defined professional/personal goals allow you to <u>keep your attention aligned with your intention.</u>

**Goal setting is a never ending process.** Remember, the two extremes to be avoided are: 1) not to have goals, and 2) to be unwilling to change goals as appropriate. Recommended reading: *Release Your Own Brakes,* by Jim Newman. This book describes a clear, easy to understand series of steps you can use to set and reach very significant goals. The strategies have enabled numerous people to reach goals they never before believed were possible.

Another critical factor in developing and maintaining ownership lies in your own *self-talk.* Self-talk is that dialogue that you have with yourself regarding what you can and cannot achieve. Often, individuals with low ownership have learned to carry on dialogue, convincing themselves of why things will not work. Monitor your negative self-talk and *change* it--focus on how things can be accomplished, not on how they cannot be.

---

' Humility should not be confused with timidness, diffidence, or lack of confidence.

**Fully accept personal responsibility** . . . you will reach your greatest levels of personal drive and resourcefulness. (It seems the rest of the world will take you seriously as soon as you are irrevocably committed to achieving your objectives.)

*Developing ownership in yourself and simultaneously in others may at times seem contradictory.* Individuals who have a high level of personal ownership have been rewarded for being accountable. Parents, teachers and supervisors have reinforced these individuals for being responsible, personal performers. They have incentive for taking ownership and getting things done themselves. This strong level of ownership may make it hard for an individual to "let go" of responsibility and transfer it to others. Sometimes these people will delegate tasks, but not the authority needed for others to take the ownership for the results. They hold onto ownership, allowing others only to act as extensions of themselves. (See *How to Manage Your Boss by Hegarty)*

**Teach your people to do their work without your ongoing participation by developing the self-esteem, competence and autonomy of every individual in your group.**

> *Exceptional leaders have a high level of personal ownership
> and simultaneously transfer ownership to others.*

**Ownership focuses a person's attention like a laser.** Research has shown that ownership impacts how a person sees the world. Each individual's "screening system" filters out information that is considered of little importance. You can achieve what is important to you by accepting ownership of what is required to achieve it. Things that you feel responsible for become important to you and get through your "screening system." This allows you to see them clearly. To a great extent this explains why a leader with high ownership can see all of the opportunities and challenges while, to their frustration, others with little ownership may "see" few or none. Transferring responsibility and accountability to others creates ownership, opens peoples' "screens" and allows them to see the problems and issues as you do.

**Exceptional leaders remain hopeful and optimistic even when it seems hopeless.**
How a person handles great crises is a clear indication of their ownership. The morning of the day after a California earthquake a live TV news team was interviewing people where property had been destroyed. They found a man in front of his home which had been reduced to rubble. The reporter asked *"How do you feel about your home being destroyed?"* The man replied *"I'm wiped out. All I've worked for is gone. I don't know what will happen to me now."* Two doors away, the news team came across another man who's home was also in ruins. The reporter again asked *"How do you feel about your home being destroyed?"* This man replied *"I would have definitely preferred that it not happen."* The reporter asked *"What will you do?"* He replied *"I will rebuild. I don't know how, but I will. You can count on that."*

What an amazing difference between the two. Which one are you most like? Real net worth is not a home, tenure, or your savings. It is an attitude of relying on yourself that you will find the answers to solve even the great crises you face. **It is a requirement all great leaders have met** and it is one you can choose for yourself by rethinking the false idea that external factors determine your real net worth.

**Developing trust in yourself, knowing you can always rely on you,
is far more critical to your success than the outcome of any one endeavor.**

---

*The measure of an exceptional leader's value is not what he or she can do personally
but what he or she can get done with others.*

---

**The highest level of leadership is when the leader is more concerned about the organization than about himself.** This could be stated *"Ask not what the organization can do for you, ask what you can do for the organization"*. This is similar to what John F. Kennedy said in 1961, *"Ask not what your country can do for you, ask what you can do for your country"*. The statement was not originated by JFK. . . it was first used in a book by Kahlil Gibran in 1915.

**Ethical leaders accept ownership at the deepest level.**
*Most people define their ethics by what they believe in and the ethics of others by their actions.* The only way to evaluate your ethics or the ethics of another person is by actions. Many people delude themselves that they are ethical even though they are not. Scan all the people you have known in good times and in bad. How many of them were ethical even when it was very difficult? If all the people who have known you in good times and in bad were to evaluate your ethics what would they say about your ethics? This is a valuable area for self evaluation.

A man and his eleven year old son stopped at the bank to cash a check. When the man recounted the money after leaving the bank, he noticed he had been given $100 too much. He said to his son, *"We've talked a lot about ethics and honesty. Here's an example: The teller accidentally gave me $100 more than the amount of the check. There is only one question we have to answer. Do we or do we not tell mom about this?"*

If this happened to you and you were certain you could get away with it, what would you do? If it were a $1,000 what would you do? If it were $10,000 what would you do ... if it were $100,000 what would you do?

**VIP:** <u>*Reflect for a moment*</u> *on how effectively you are using the opposite pages to record your thoughts, questions, insights and plans about how you will apply the material from this program.*

# EMPATHY

*"Empathy is the precursor of rapport."*
*-William Soroka*

Empathy is the ability to understand others. Exceptional leaders learn to relate to all types of people and they develop the skills to build and maintain a team effort. They understand what makes both individuals and groups want to succeed. They quickly develop and maintain the rapport and trust necessary to create *"competitive collaboration"* whereby individuals compete and cooperate simultaneously.

To move team members to higher levels of performance it is necessary to understand who each person is in terms of background, interests, competence and values. An *Exceptional Leader* works diligently to understand the group as a whole and each person individually. Leaders who lack the skill or interest to do this tend to create a communication cycle of resistance, resentment and revenge. On the other hand, when you interact with others in an empathetic, respectful way, you build a communication cycle based on clarity, cooperation and commitment. Exceptional Leaders develop high levels of rapport and trust with their people.
**When necessary . . . they accept being disliked and misunderstood to get the job done.**

*Exceptional leaders not only have the ability to communicate the "co-vision" clearly, but are also successful in dealing with the group as a whole and with the individual members on a one-to-one basis.* People respond to empathic leadership by becoming more competitive and cooperative simultaneously. They strive individually to do their jobs better and, at the same time, reach out to help others in the group.

*Put your people on your shoulders--help them reach beyond you--that is the role of a leader.*

The dynamics of a particular group is a direct reflection of the relationship between the leader and the group. When working with leaders I can often define their group without meeting them. When working with groups, I can frequently define their leaders without meeting them.

Building an exceptional team requires accurately assessing the talents of individuals and then knowing how to effectively utilize those talents alongside the talents of other team members. Exceptional leaders have learned how to select highly appropriate individuals who are ideally suited to perform the jobs the leader needs done. Many organizations both large and small have no real idea of how to identify top job candidates.

Phil Nelson has seen numerous organizations carefully evaluate capital investments in new equipment, offices, etc., and then casually make key personnel decisions. He teaches client organizations to exercise the same degree of disciplined evaluation in the selection of people as they do in other areas. Many of the organizations that follow his selection strategies have reduced turnover and increased productivity.[+]

---

[+] See *Position Suitablity Profile System,* by Philip Nelson.

In this time when leadership is more exciting, exacting and challenging than ever before you need the support of everyone in your group. Tom Haggai, author of *How The Best Is Won*, emphasizes the importance of selecting the right players and then creating an intelligent action plan to develop them. The exceptional leader fosters action, independence and interdependence in team members. Train your people to stand on their own and rise, in a relentlessly competent, decisive way, to the day-to-day challenges facing them. Teach them how to think and how to be autonomous, in order to achieve the organization's goals, in their *own* way for their *own* reasons.

In his book, *Inspiring People in the Workplace,* management consultant Jan Kantor cautions *"Never take relationships for granted. When under relentless challenge many leaders forget how valuable their people are and treat them in a manner you would never treat a stranger."*

Know your team members and your customers. Today it is not an option . . . it is a requirement!

**Use the best management consultants in the world . . . your team members and your clients.** They hold the potential to help your organization succeed on a long-term basis. Create strategies to communicate clearly with them that will cause them to participate with you. They may hold the difference between failure and success for your organization. Recommended reading: *Up the Loyalty Ladder* by Murray and Neil Raphel.

The dramatic personal and work-values revolution that a large part of the world is undergoing is much more significant than most people realize. This will require leaders to understand and deal effectively with *very* diverse groups of people. Customers and employees alike require ever higher levels of understanding.

*Listen respectfully to others . . . evaluate their advice carefully . . . when appropriate, act on it.*

**_The more responsibility is given to individuals the greater the need for strong leadership._** Giving employees responsibility for their own work does not mean the leader abdicates the role of leader. It does mean the leader plays a different role. Instead of issuing orders the leader creates rapport and trust with all the people in the group by being a superb listener and by dealing with everybody in the group as individuals. *They compete and cooperate simultaneously.*
*The leader causes them to function as a team . . . not just on a team.*

To be effective today a leader must be:

    **1) forceful** . . . have high levels of drive
    **2) focused** . . . communicate crystal clear objectives understood by all
    **3) flexible** . . . be willing to change whenever necessary
    **4) fair** . . . treat everybody as a distinct and valuable individual.

Contrary to what many claim, a leader need not be charitable, loving or sympathetic.

*The real secret to effective performance is to make individuals responsible for their work.*

> *The goal of most leaders is to cause people to feel reverence for the leader.*
>
> *The goal of the exceptional leader is to cause people to feel reverence for themselves..*

There are many things you can accomplish on your own. The great artist, musician, or athlete can refine and develop skills and fulfill dreams without help from others. They can also get away with eccentric behavior a leader could most often not. For example, Beethoven while working would go for weeks without washing or changing clothes and would scream at everyone in sight. For most of us, however, our accomplishments hinge on how successful we are in enlisting others to help us.

A challenge that you may face is that you've reached where you are because of intense personal efforts and performance. You've been rewarded throughout your career for getting things done by yourself. As a consequence, you may not have seen the *value* or *need* to learn how to *listen to* and *understand* others. In order to go from where you are to where you would now like to be requires that you *shift gears* and learn the skills necessary to work *with* and *through* people.

Remember the example of Warren Gregory--after learning how to be an outstanding achiever he shifted gears and also learned to be an outstanding leader.

**Empathy is a skill you *can* develop**. It is an emotional intelligence factor. Take training in Active Listening. It is a required leadership skill. Interview people about their values, concerns, hopes, and approaches. Gain insight into how and why people do what they do. Grasp every opportunity to talk with or listen to people different from you. This will help you understand how to lead a diverse group. Well written books, including novels, allow you to vicariously learn about people. Position yourself to understand those around you. What is important to them? What are their values and their hopes? How do they think? What do they feel? Take the time to ask questions and listen carefully. Involve yourself in debates in which you take the opposite side of issues you now believe in order to gain insight. Through this process you will understand how others deal with the people and the events of their lives. Show others you care by participating with them in this fashion. This will cause them to want to join your team.

We live and work in a time of a personal and a work values revolution in which people are becoming less alike and more individualized. It is now more critical than ever to be able to empathize. Being a superb listener enables you to learn what will cause people to want to work and perform for *their* reasons. This may often differ from the ones that drive or motivate you.

Today's leaders are required to deal with people who are culturally, socially and ethnically very different from one another. A study at SRI International has identified nine separate and distinctive groups of men and women in America today, each group with values and interests different from the others, and many of them are people you will be required to deal with. Understand your people as individuals; their lives, values, hopes, skills, talents and drives. By understanding them as a group and individually you can then organize them into high performance teams, where the abilities of the individuals contribute so that the whole is truly more than a sum of the parts. It is an actual act of synergy.

**Committed team members simultaneously cooperate and compete with each other.**

Change does not occur spontaneously. It almost always occurs in response to a new challenge or demand. A leader cannot simply expect people to develop, but must assist them to grow in competence and stature.

A yearly performance appraisal, where a few development needs are pointed out, is no longer sufficient (actually, it never was). Instead of looking at people as pawns to be shifted and moved in a large chess game, exceptional leaders recognize the importance of every individual's professional and personal growth and development. Your success as an exceptional leader will come from motivating and enabling your people to achieve for their own reasons. Phil Nelson shows organizations how to precisely evaluate a person's potential by clearly understanding the person's experiences, talents, values, temperament and deep seated attitudes and beliefs.

Some leaders are threatened by people whom they perceive as highly talented and may intentionally or unintentionally hold them back, exceptional leaders, however, know that they are only as good as the team they can assemble. They enable others to continuously increase their autonomy, competence, and self-esteem. *Have your people try new ways . . . explore new territories . . . take intelligent risks . . . continuously improve.*

**Exceptional leaders** may sometimes have a high rate of turnover among their people. However, unlike poor leaders who have a high rate of turnover because of problems, exceptional leaders turn people over who are moving upward because of increased competence. They create a high performance group with many people wanting to join and they take pride in having people go on to greater responsibilities.

There is an amazing contrast between an organization with a leader and a group of passive followers and one in which the leader is developing and releasing the talents and skills of all the team members. The ultimate way that a group can perform is when exceptional leadership is demonstrated by the leader and also by the ever more competent subordinates. It becomes a magnificent circle of progress. **Subordinates learn to lead -the leader learns to follow.**

DO NOT CONFUSE EMPATHY WITH SYMPATHY. To understand and respect others' viewpoints does not mean to be wrongly swayed by them. Your commitment to your vision will often be challenged. Be unwavering in the pursuit of your goals.

Empathy allows you to create high levels of rapport and trust with each of the individuals in your group. Without this critical skill, the vast majority of your people will not offer ideas or solutions that vary with what they perceive is your viewpoint. They have learned through experience that in most circumstances it is better to not "rock the boat." Exceptional leaders require people to speak up so as to avoid a "Poseidon Adventure." There are powerful practical techniques that dramatically increase an individual's willingness to "tell it the way it really is"

---

See *Integrated Management Development System,* by Philip Nelson.
See *How to Manage Your Boss,* by Christopher Hegarty.

# A MAJOR CAUSE OF FAILURE

*Ongoing studies confirm that more than 75% of people in most organizations will not be candid with their boss. They have "learned" that it is not safe to tell the truth. Many of their comments, actions and strategies are primarily based on their desire for political survival.*

**Organizations have suffered, in some cases perished, because individuals did not feel safe in speaking up.**

At a speaking assignment for a worldwide corporation I was scheduled to follow the executive in charge of the group. During his talk he told a story about a recent hire who told him most of his people were afraid to speak to him openly. . . especially about bad news. He said to the group *"Please know I want to speak at any time with anyone who has a concern or a good idea."* He then asked if there were any questions. In the back of the room I could feel fear in the group. I opened my presentation by saying that I had a strong sense that there were pressing questions not asked. After my presentation one of the attendees whispered to me *"You were totally right about the questions. We don't know what is safe to say and until we do we won't say anything."*
Make certain this is not the case in your group.

## *The very survival of your group may be determined by whether your people tell you the truth.*

**Take nothing for granted.** *Develop trust and rapport with your people.* Do not delude yourself as to how you're doing with your people (as most leaders do). Take risks and use intelligent strategies (ask questions, actively listen, etc.) to know exactly how you are doing. It's risky to be vulnerable . . . but then to be a leader today requires taking risks. Astrophysicist Michael Munn says *"It is possible to send a message to the moon in an instant, yet it often takes years to convey a message to someone you see every day."* Munn should know. . . he is a rocket scientist turned personal development seminar leader.

**The higher up you are in an organization the less direct feedback you get about your performance, and the more at risk you are to be released without any advance opportunity to make corrections.** Remember, how you evaluate your performance is not nearly as vital to your future success as how others evaluate your performance. Respectfully ask for input from others on how you can do your job better (see page 53). They can assist you in maximizing your strengths and minimizing your weaknesses.

*The number one cause of leader failure is lack of interpersonal skills,*
*regardless of the intelligence, technical knowledge and experience of a leader . . .*
*if the leader cannot communicate effectively he or she will almost certainly fail.*

## Managing Cultural Diversity

Bob Abramms, former CEO of ODT has had extensive experience dealing with communication challenges in diverse work groups. Here's what he says about it:

*"Managing requires a broader set of empathetic skills than it did 25 years ago. Today we are required to communicate effectively with people cross-culturally, through the generation gap, among races, between genders, and across those subtle but pervasive barriers of class. No wonder it may make us feel uncomfortable--we've never been asked to do this before!"*

*"Unconsciously, although understandably enough, most of us hold the notion that our own reality is the only real one and that anything that doesn't comfortably fit within it is wrong, bad, unworkable or alien. At best, differences in others from this perspective are perceived as being irritating or inconvenient. The exceptional leader strives to empathize and understand people who might have a vastly different set of life experiences."*

### Here's how to find out how your people see you as a leader.

If your goal is to be the best leader you are capable of being, learn how to clearly understand the impact of your leadership on other people. The way to discover how your people view you as a leader is to ask them. This is a radical and sometimes unacceptable idea for many in leadership. It does contain risks . . . you may find out some things about your leadership you do not like . . . an even greater risk is that you may discover things about yourself as a person that you do not like. However, the willingness to change may hold enormous benefit for you as a leader and as a person.

I once asked an executive how his people viewed him as a leader. He replied, *"They see me kind of like a friendly uncle."* I asked him to run an anonymous survey to see if he was right. He called me in a few days and said, *"Chris, my people think I am a barbarian."* Since his desire was to be a more empathetic leader, he set out to create mutual support agreements (see next page) with each member of his staff. He learned a great deal about his strengths and weaknesses and found that there were changes he was willing to make. In less than a year the performance output of his group dramatically improved. Additionally, he was under a lot less stress and for the first time in his work experience was enjoying being a leader.

> *Learning what your people really think is required. If your people will not level with you, your effectiveness will be dramatically-- perhaps even fatally-- hampered.*

A major consequence of poor communication is people often harm their boss or their organization. Revenge in the workplace is dramatically increasing. The case of an executive at a major US company who secretly recorded fellow executives discussing how to destroy evidence related to a discrimination lawsuit is an example of workplace revenge.

---

For a free copy of *Dealing with Diversity: Playing Straight with a Mixed Deck*, write ODT, Box 134, Amherst, MA., 01004.

# CREATE MUTUAL SUPPORT AGREEMENTS

excerpted from *How to Manage Your Boss,* by Christopher Hegarty

**Support . . . Do not criticize.** Bosses and subordinates are both ideally situated to spot weak points in each other's performance; they often see ways in which the other can improve. The problem comes when those ideas are expressed in the form of criticism. Sometimes, sound ideas that the person could benefit from are never put to use because they were improperly conveyed.

*Constructive criticism is almost always destructive. Even well-intentioned criticism can be destructive, because what really matters is how the person receiving the criticism experiences it-not what the criticizer's intention is. So, even if your intention is to help, it is not effective if the person feels put down or diminished by your criticism.*

*In our leadership seminars, I often ask the audience: "How many of you use constructive criticism with your subordinates?" Almost everyone raises his or her hand. Then I ask: "How many of you enjoy receiving constructive criticism?" Hardly any hands go up. "That," I say, "is how much your people enjoy criticism."*

*Although I never liked to be criticized myself, I used "constructive criticism" as a way of getting people to do things the way I felt they should be done. I had no alternative. Then, during a discussion with one of my executives, my criticism turned the meeting into a violent argument. Leaving the office with my stomach in knots, I suddenly saw another way. It has since worked well for me and many others. It is called the "mutual support agreement." Here is how I used it after that violent argument.*

*I explained to each person who worked for me: "I'd like you to know that for as long as we work together, you have my permission and my encouragement to comment on how I can be a more effective executive. If we work in a mutually supportive manner, helping each other improve our work, we will each benefit."*

*Because I was seen as a criticizer, it took some time before they accepted the idea. Each time I worked with one of them, I would conclude by asking for ideas on how I could improve my performance. The feedback I received enabled me to see certain of my weaknesses for the first time and it showed me I had strengths that I had neither understood nor utilized. I quickly became a more effective leader. After four or five such meetings, most of them felt comfortable enough to ask me how they could improve their performance.*

*The entire context of our relationship changed. Now each meeting consisted of two people raising their own self-esteem and working out ways for each to be more competent. Our individual and group productivity improved substantially. We had replaced criticism with mutual support and could now be competitive and cooperative simultaneously.*

*We now functioned <u>as</u> a team . . . not just <u>on</u> a team.*

*With a mutual support agreement, each person's suggestions are supported by the other person. It gives each person not only the right but the responsibility to comment on how the other's performance can be improved. Mutual trust, respect and cooperation will be established and continually enhanced. If you are in charge of others, carefully create mutual support agreement with each of them individually. Attempt to establish a mutual support agreement with your boss as well. If you handle it creatively and responsibly, you will find your boss's feedback more agreeable and you will be able to improve your boss's effectiveness as well as your own, in a way that you will both value.*

# HOLD REVERSE STAFF MEETINGS

excerpted from *How To Manage Your Boss,* by Christopher Hegarty

*Reverse staff meetings are a powerful tool to build empathy for everybody in the group, including the leader. In a reverse staff meeting, the leader doesn't have a cast-iron agenda. He uses a "meeting process" in which everyone else's interests and concerns are revealed. Responsibility for the meeting is equally distributed. If it runs too long, or if important issues are not covered, all participants share the responsibility; if it runs well, everyone shares the credit.*

*The leader announces at the outset that the format will be different, and that everyone is responsible for making the meeting work. The leader tells everyone that candor and honesty will be appreciated, and that no one will be punished or criticized. Then the leader should begin by asking one person a question, such as: "Since our last meeting, what has been going on in your area that has worked well?" Or: "What has held you back from getting the job done?" Other questions might be: "What have I done that has helped?" "What have I done that has hindered your work?" "What should I have done more of?" "What conflicts do you have with me?"*

*There are numerous benefits to be gained from reverse staff meetings: hidden agendas, resentments and hostilities that prevent meetings from working are eliminated; the responsibility for the meeting is evenly distributed; if there is a saboteur in the group, his or her power is neutralized. . .when colleagues know the saboteur can speak freely in a meeting, they will not be influenced by destructive talk at other times.*

*The first few times reverse meetings are held, your people may feel awkward. However, once they learn they can tell the truth without reprisal, they will speak out. This format is a powerful tool for improving communication and cooperation, and it requires a leader with self-esteem and a willingness to take risks. If you are easily embarrassed, or if you would be threatened by hearing comments about how you might improve, use these meetings carefully or not at all. While they should not be used on occasions when the leader has a clear-cut agenda of items to cover, there are many times when a regular gathering can be turned into a reverse staff meeting, if you are willing to take the risk.*

*You can earn your boss's (if you have one) respect by having him or her witness an exceptional meeting for which you are responsible. Prepare for the occasion in advance. Work out the kinks in several other meetings before your boss attends--"Don't open on Broadway." Prepare your boss by revealing the nature of the meeting and its purpose. Prepare the participants by telling them that the boss will be attending, and what the boss's role will be. That role should be either participant or observer, depending on which is appropriate.*

*When the day arrives, your boss will be impressed by seeing a group of highly responsible people deal competently with solutions, not just problems, relating to reality, not just personalities. Goals should be clearly established, along with precise methods for accomplishing them and ways to measure results. Well-organized visual aids such as slides, charts and graphs can add value and interest. So will imaginative additions like a significant guest speaker. A sales manager for a carpet manufacturer invited the vice president of sales to an important meeting, where she had a guest speaker--the purchasing agent from a large hotel chain that was a valued customer. The sales manager who organized the meeting rose in stature as a result; she was invited to serve on the company's meeting committee for its annual conference, a boost to her credibility and visibility. The purchasing agent who spoke gave valuable insights to the group and increased his carpet purchases.*

# STRATEGIES FOR CHANGE

### *Turn your back to change and it will hit you in your <u>Assets</u>.*

To help develop your leadership skills, let's take a candid look at change and its implications for you as both an individual and as a leader helping those around you to change.

### We are in a race that has no finish line.

**We will never again see a time when the status quo is not changing.** Every profession, industry, group and individual will deal with ever increasing rates of change. Today, the average person entering our work force will likely undergo seven career changes (not job changes).

Despite all of the rhetoric about change, many individuals and some entire organizations are not facing the needed changes. Even when evidence proves it is better to change, many stay with the way they originally learned how to do things. *They harm themselves and their organizations by <u>resorting to the familiar</u> at the very time they must find new ways of getting the job done.*

Author William Morin in *Silent Sabotage* claims that a survey of Michigan manufacturing company CEOs found that over 90% of them viewed their employees as liabilities, not assets. What a difficult mindset they have in dealing with their people. If the employees know how they are viewed, it is even more dangerous to the future of these firms. It will be very difficult for these firms to make the changes necessary for their survival, not to mention their success.

Change is often difficult, it requires commitment and sometimes courage. However . . .

### REFUSING TO CHANGE IS LIKE REFUSING TO BREATHE . . . DIFFICULT AT THE OUTSET AND EVENTUALLY IMPOSSIBLE.

The ever accelerating rate of change will create ever more exciting and challenging events. You will likely be faced almost daily with "wall to wall" challenges.

- ♦ **If you see these challenges as wall to wall <u>problems</u>, it will be a daily battle.**

- ♦ **If you see them as wall to wall <u>opportunities</u>, it will be a daily adventure.**

> *It is estimated that 4% of people are willing to look at new realities, accept the need to change, and risk making the changes; the other 96% will do everything they can to keep things from being different. Which one are you?*

Remember Vincent Stroops who lived to be 101 and remained a young, flexible, learning person all of his life. He lived by five principles of wisdom. His principle in reference to change was *"I accepted everything life dealt me including those things I would have gladly given my life to have missed."* He taught me how to look wisely at changes that I could not control. He said, *"Chris, capitalize on all unwanted changes you cannot control by altering your viewpoint about them."*
***Only fools of the highest order resist or resent changes that are beyond their control.***

*Your view of challenges you face will greatly influence the outcome.* There are four different ways to view them - as an **optimist, skeptic, pessimist, or cynic.** Which is the ideal way?

William James, the father of modern psychology said, *"The only thing worst than a pessimist is an optimist."* His statement is both accurate and inaccurate. To be blindly optimistic, seeing the world through rose colored glasses, is naive and recklessly dangerous. Skepticism is often used to squelch good ideas. **Pessimism and cynicism are self inflicted acts of personal violence.** What then is the ideal attitude? It is to be an optimist who requires proof to support ideas and claims. Be open-minded to the possibilities and set up the standards to prove or disprove the idea. A review of history shows that you should never bet against the optimists. I have never met a successful pessimistic entrepreneur or sales person. Psychologist Martin Seligman of Harvard states, *"Research shows that optimists bounce back after failures while pessimists often see their failures as permanent."*

---

*Optimists are determined to find opportunities in difficulties . . . pessimists and cynics are determined to find difficulties in opportunities.*

---

**Do not get trapped into believing there are final answers or only one way to do things.**
A very powerful block to effective leadership is denying reality. Many leaders imperil their organization by refusing to acknowledge the need to change and organizations have perished because their leaders were unwilling or unable to be ruthlessly honest about the changes needed.

**While moving forward with their plans in place, exceptional leaders remain in a perpetual state of readiness, prepared to immediately make any and all necessary changes.**

**The Future Belongs to the Omnicompetent.**
In addition to the hardware and software necessary in a high tech world there are two other ingredients that must be understood. The first is **brainware**; the intelligence which is used to look at all the changes taking place and how to capitalize on them. The second is **heartware**; applying compassion and understanding to your organization's long range decisions and their consequences.

*In the late 60s Swiss Watch manufacturers controlled over 60% of the worldwide watch market. With the advent of Quartz technology, Seiko and Texas Instruments raced to the market and the Swiss watch manufacturers fell to less than 8% of the worldwide market. The most startling part of this is that the Swiss Watch Research Institute originated the quartz technology. Their "experience" prevented them from properly assessing the value of their own discovery and they gave away their future.*

**Every generation claims to be the most challenged.** The truth is that this is the first generation to have lived when we have visited another planet. It is the first generation where destructive power has been developed to the point where it can end the world. However, there is a new kind of struggle now between countries - economic warfare. The focus of all industrial countries is to create a prominent place for themselves in this new rapidly changing world wide economic reality wherein competition is ever more challenging and the world ever more complex. The Swiss watch manufacturers are a classic example of a group that couldn't see past their traditional ways of thinking and doing things. It was many years before the Swiss companies recaptured a significant market share with Swatch watches. From now on . . . **it will often be fatal for groups to be blind to new ways of thinking and doing.**

In our seminar, *Fiscal Fitness for Organizations*, we show business owners how to reduce their operating overhead (in some cases dramatically) without ever paying a fee or causing any disruption. *For many firms it will mean the difference between survival and failure.*
As hard as this may be to believe, only 10 percent act on it.

There are a variety of reasons why people resist change. Among them are:

♦ They are afraid of the implications of change (loss of identity).

♦ They are frightened of losing control (disruption of long standing routines).

♦ They are short-term oriented and cannot see past the next dividend.

♦ They have no idea how to prepare for change.

♦ They view their competence by their current skills rather than by learning new ones.

♦ Their organization offers no intelligent assistance to help them change.

Biologically, we each have *"comfort zone set points."* A process called homeostasis is designed to keep an individual in a biological steady state. When we think of normal blood pressure, normal blood chemistry, normal temperature, etc., it is the process of homeostasis within our body that is working automatically to keep us within our comfort zone set points.

Psychologically, we also have homeostasis and comfort zones. Once you have formulated many of your habits and beliefs, they become your normal state. It is the process of homeostasis that allows you to get up in the morning and act like yourself without thinking about it. It is also homeostasis, the "set points" in our attitudes, that can impede change. We each have ways of dealing with situations and people, and ways of thinking about challenges that "are the way do it." It is these "comfort zone set points" that may keep us from changing.

**Be respectful of the process of change.** Major changes (as determined by the viewpoint of the individual) are sometimes as impactful as the loss of a loved one. The steps necessary to deal with major changes are 1) shock, 2) denial, 3) anger, 4) depression, 5) acceptance. Acknowl-edging and honoring this process can help a person make the changes with less fear and stress.

♦ *It is much easier to create an attitude than it is to change an already existing attitude . . . focus on creating the correct attitudes in yourself and others right from the start. It is often easier to do better with new people than it is with those who have been with the organization a long time.*

♦ *Experience is not always the best teacher.* Many people want to stay with the way it's always been done. **Sometimes experience is the worst teacher.** *Experience often makes a person or an entire organization resistant to new ways of doing things.* You can change by "reframing" the way you see yourself and your organization.

---

| **Remember:  you can no more ignore the force of change than you can the force of gravity.** |
| --- |

---

Contact us for a complimentary copy of *Fiscal Fitness for Organizations.*

Here are some strategies:

♦ Recognize the limiting power of *"comfort zone set points"* and how they are linked to your attitudes, habits and beliefs.

♦ Jump out of your comfort zone by thinking and acting in new ways. Experience different ways of doing things, new ways of thinking and evaluating. Expose yourself to new life styles. Talk to and interact with people different from you.

♦ Re-think every area of your life. Create and implement new approaches.

♦ Do emergency fire drills. Act as if you were experiencing new crises.

> *One of our clients "imagined" losing their largest customer. The customer represented 40% of gross sales. The client immediately took steps to reduce the dangerous dependence on one customer. There is now no customer that represents more than 18% of gross sales.*

♦ Continuously expand your versatility and vulnerability. A bungee jump would indicate how willing you are to experience being out of control.

♦ Unlearn values, concepts and ideas that prevent you from moving to a new place.

*Stand apart from the crowd . . . let your mind show in public. Tell it as you see it.*
Many people, by age seven, have determined what they believe in, and what they are and are not capable of. They have become "victims of coincidence." They spend their lives not questioning, but following what they learned as youngsters--religion, prejudice, belief about success, etc. Recommended reading *If It Ain't Broke ...BREAK IT!* by Robert Kriegel.

**Context is more important than content in enabling people to change**. A yet unknown fact to enable people to change is to focus on how they view the changes. Rather than attempting to change their behavior, you will be far more successful showing them how to change context. *Content is the behavior required to change. Context is the viewpoint the person has about the needed change.* (See page 53 for a powerful proven technique to change context.) In our seminars, we use a number of whole brain thinking strategies to enable people to quickly alter their awareness and change their viewpoint about the necessary changes. A person's level of awareness is what determines their behavior. For example, many people agree with the fact they should be computer literate but feel overwhelmed by the awesome task of developing the necessary skills. Their viewpoint is that they were born too late or thought they could get by without doing it, etc. By applying various whole brain thinking strategies, they can quickly change their behavior by altering their awareness to see the challenge as an exciting, vitally important opportunity to increase their competence.

Like many, I was convinced there was no need for me to be computer literate (my staff is) or go on-line. While visiting a friend, I asked him what he knew about Ethiopia. He said, *"nothing."* His son Trenton said, *"I can help you."* He turned on his computer, put in a CD ROM and within seconds a map of Ethiopia appeared on the screen. He said *"What would you like to know? The form of government? The prevailing religion? The health standards?"* I was stunned. Trenton was six years old. My viewpoint changed on the spot. I instantly realized I had become functionally illiterate. In a matter of months, I had a site on the World Wide Web and now do business on the Internet. I am currently using more advanced computer technology than Trenton, even though he is now seven. With 20 hours training, you can learn all that is required.

**Re-think everything you believe, everything you do, continuously.**

- Be willing to make very unpopular decisions . . . if you are convinced they're needed.

- Do not pursue popularity. Pursue trust and respect.

- Listen to others' ideas carefully and respectfully and use their input when appropriate.

- Whether you're doing well or not, make changes and improve your organization and yourself.

- Change your appearance. Get a new look. (Three out of four men wear dress shirts with the neck size at least one size too small, so they do not get enough blood to the brain. If all the men in the US would wear the right size shirt, it would cause a measurable increase in our nation's productivity). Get a new style haircut, different clothing. You can dress tastefully without wearing the traditional look.

To change your organization, change your mind about how you see it--cause your people to change by involving them in changes at the outset. Do it right and they will help make the changes. *Keep your group in a state of "Creative Discomfort --change and change again--keep in practice.*

## YEARS LIVED IS NOT THE MAJOR FACTOR IN CHANGEABILITY

*What is your mental and emotional age? This is much more important than chronological age.*

There are many examples where "old dogs have learned new tricks." Many CEOs past the traditional age of retirement have guided their firms through great changes and then retired, only to come out of retirement to lead other organizations during times of even greater change. . .with extraordinary success. They are lifelong learners. On the other hand, there are many CEOs in their thirties and forties who are already old . . . rigid . . . arbitrary . . . unwilling to change . . . Recommended reading: *The Six Steps to the Fountain of Youth,* by Dennis Kelly.

PETER DRUCKER at age 89 was recently selected by Forbes Magazine as the single best thinker alive on management and business. His current views prove that his mind remains profoundly insightful. The story of how he came to be the person he is should be required reading for all in leadership. It is impossible to read Drucker and not learn. My observation about Drucker is:
*"Drucker says more in a single statement than most business thinkers could say in a lifetime."*

M.B. "DUKE" RUDMAN is a philanthropist and business man. He founded a highly successful independent oil company specializing in wildcat drilling. He sold his holdings in the 1970s and then decided to start all over again. Today at the age of 86 he is drilling more wildcats and is more successful then ever before in his 55 years of business. When he was 72 he and Andy Kaye were the world Frontennis doubles champions. He is also an award winning inspirational speaker who is credited by many people as the reason for their success.

LEO KAHN co-founded Fresh Fields grocery market chain at the age of 73. His firm was so successful selling organic produce and healthy food it was selected as grocer of the year in 1994. Now 80 he very recently sold his interest in the company to launch yet another enterprise.

LOREN DUNTON was in his 50's when he founded the enormously successful International Association for Financial Planning. In his late 60's he founded the National Center for Financial Education. As a result of his efforts millions of Americans are creating a brighter future for themselves and their families. Now nearly 80 he is still the head of the NCFE, writing books and traveling internationally as a sought after speaker. He created two valuable non-profit organizations at great financial sacrifice to himself. He is a genuine American hero.

DR. VALERIE HUNT, a professor and physiological scientist, retired after 35 years at UCLA and is currently launching a major new research laboratory on the atomic energy patterns in the body preceding physical and emotional disorders. At age 80, she is still a world traveler and lecturer and has recently published 3 books.

MAYO KAAN was selected as the first Superman at age 22 in 1936 by the originators of the concept. He had just recovered from a spinal injury (semi-pro football) his doctors said would cause permanent paralysis. He turned down the chance to play Superman in the movies because of his interest in helping others with health problems. He and his wife have operated a health clinic/gym for more than fifty years. Today at age 82 he is in superb condition and still helping people. He recently found the original Superman photos and is selling prints (888-387-8737) with a percentage of all sales going to Christopher Reeve's charity to help paralysis victims.

ROBERT AUSTIN was a successful sales executive through his entire business career. He retired in his late sixties but always maintained a keen interest in business. Seeing exciting new opportunities in the changing business world he recently returned to the field of business and today at the age of 81 he is again in the ranks of top performing sales executives.

It is neccesary to think younger. Retirement age will be moved to 75 to prolong Social Security.

**Changeability is not determined by chronological age. . .it is determined by mental and emotional age.** Here's an interesting way to help you define your age:

> *"Youth is not a time of life--it is a state of mind.* *It is not a matter of rosy cheeks, red lips and supple knees; it is an attitude, a quality of the imagination, a vigor of the emotions. Youth means a predominance of courage over timidity, a preference for adventure over love of ease. Years wrinkle the skin, but to give up enthusiasm wrinkles the soul. Whether seventy or seventeen, there can be in every being's heart a sense of wonder, the sweet amazement at the stars, the challenge of new events, childlike curiosity, and the joy of living. You are as young as your faith, as old as your doubt; as young as your self-confidence, as old as your fear; as young as your hope, as old as your despair. So long as your heart is warmed by the messages of beauty, hope, cheer, courage, and meaning in life, you will remain young."*
>
> *-Anonymous*

---

**There is no valid reason to accept the commonly held belief that there is a predetermined time in a person's life in which he or she is too old to reach demanding goals personally or professionally**

# MAKING CHANGES

*"Only when your <u>intellectual knowledge</u> is also <u>integrated at the feeling level</u>*
*and*
*<u>expressed through your behavior</u> do you fully understand how to change."*

*Carl Jung*

**Knowing what changes have to be made is not sufficient to make them.**  Most people will stay with what is familiar, even if there is abundant evidence that it is not working.  Predictability and familiarity are mistaken for comfort and safety.  Exceptional leaders  continuously make changes.

Creating and capitalizing on change in your attitudes, beliefs and habits causes "creative discomfort," which help you to remain competent.  Giving in to your comfort zone, on the other hand, can seem to be very non-threatening.  The decision to change or be changed is yours.  **Remember, context is more vital than content.**

Many people, even very young adults have retired on active duty, hoping the old familiar ways will continue to work, even when there is abundant proof that many of the old ways have to be changed.  Change does not come *easily*.  Old habits die hard.  It generally requires hard work.

## Avoid The Disease Of Being Right

At the peak of his fame, Albert Einstein was asked during an interview, *"How do you feel, knowing so many people are trying to prove you are not right?"*  Einstein replied. *"I have no interest whatsoever in being right, I am only interested in finding out whether or not I am right."*  What a role-model he is for today's leader. He was humble and had a highly evolved ego.

**Practice zero-based thinking.  Look at everything you do, as if you had never seen it before, and ask questions . . .** *Why is this being done?  Is it vital?  Can it be improved?  Can it be eliminated? What would we do if we couldn't do it this way?*

Every organization, regardless of a one-person shop or a world-wide enterprise, has opportunities on a continuous basis to innovate and improve.  Find the ones in your organization and take advantage of them.

*Approach all changes with confidence and humility.*

**More than 75% of all attempted major changes fail.**  *To succeed at making significant changes requires extraordinary planning, masterful execution, continuous attention and relentless devotion.*

The cover story of  Inc. Magazine, June 1995, "The Open Book Revolution" catalogs the immense number of failures.  It also cites the fact that many people have been deeply disappointed by following the book of the month on management and leadership changes. Their belief is that the <u>open book method</u> is the best way to achieve successful long term changes.

**This approach requires courage to implement. There are four steps required:**

*1) Full disclosure. Tell your people <u>everything</u> about your organization, the good and the bad.*

*2) Teach the basic principles of business to all employees. Be sure every employee is aware of the cost of every component of doing business and can read and thoroughly understand the organization's financial statement.*

*3) Delegate responsibility/ authority and control to the people doing the work.*

*4) Involve everyone in the risks and the successes. The income of every employee goes up or down based on the on-going performance of all employees.*

A significant number of organizations that have used the *open book method* successfully found that implementing it transformed the thinking of all the people from entry level employees to top management.

Insight, courage, thoughtfulness and commitment are necessary to use this extraordinary strategy. Far better to not do it than to do it half-heartedly.

## One of the best kept secrets in American business: The Scanlon Plan

It is crucial that all members of your group be deeply involved in creating and carrying out your organization's plans. The Scanlon Plan Associates, headquartered in Lansing, Michigan, is a unique nonprofit organization devoted to teaching companies how to involve every person in the creation and execution of innovative solutions to competitive challenges. In the Scanlon plan, a share of the measurable increases in financial profits is shared with the workers. Four of the Scanlon Plan Associates member companies are listed in the latest edition of *The 100 Best Companies to Work For In America.* A recent study shows that the **member firms succeed in making major changes 66% of the time, while the national average is less than 25%.** The Scanlon Plan is indeed one of the best kept secrets in American business. Every company using it properly has had dramatic, measurable improvement in productivity and profitability. We highly recommend it.

Notice the similarities with the *open book method.* A number of the Scanlon Plan clients use the open book method. Recommended reading: *The Power of Open Book Management*, by Schuster, Carpenter & Kane.

## A word of warning

If you plan to implement major changes watch out for one of the seven neurotic leadership blocks....The Need To Resist Reality. Intellectual integrity is what Drucker calls a leader's willingness to see things the way they are, not the way the leader wants them to be. For a leader to practice intellectual integrity requires ruthless self honesty, the willingness to make mistakes and the capacity to change them without ego embarrassment.

Today it is a requirement to successfully build an organization. **Are you ready?**

# WATCH OUT FOR YOUR EGO!

**Fear of Failure and Fear of Success are Ego Fears.** Many people never attempt to be a leader because of fear of failure. Many others never succeed as a leader because of fear of success. Both of these most powerful fears are ego fears. A leader with the fear of failure lives in constant emotional turmoil. A leader with the fear of success sabotages his activities just before they are about to pay off. Both of these fears, most often unconscious, can be easily corrected with new breakthroughs in skill training. An exceptionally bright executive I know had an unconscious fear of success. I observed him destroy two separate enterprises just as they were about to succeed. After working with him to eliminate the fear of success, his third enterprise was an enormous success. People with the fear of failure and the fear of success can eliminate it and become very effective leaders. It is not difficult to identify and correct these fears.

**Many organizations have been destroyed by the ego wars of the people who work there.** *The individuals view each other as adversaries rather than allies.* They are more devoted to harming each other than helping the organization succeed. This internal warfare is a greater threat to the organization than any external forces. I personally watched one of the all time great airlines destroyed by the primitive egos of some of the operating executives.

**It takes a strong ego to be an effective leader; however there are two kinds of egos . . . <u>primitive</u> and <u>evolved</u>.** Many bright people with primitive egos tend to kneel at their own altar. They set out to prove themselves right rather than evaluate a situation honestly. Too often they bring a cloud of preconceived notions. They are blinded by their ego. The price they and others pay for this blindness is incalculable. While no one likes to accept the blame when something goes wrong, a person with a primitive ego will search for a scapegoat.

I once did a series of assignments for a very large conglomerate. The executives I worked with kept me away from the CEO of the parent firm because he had a massive primitive ego and was often brutal in dealing with people. On one occasion, to keep him from coming to my meeting, a helicopter was chartered to fly him to a new plant during the time I was speaking to the leaders of all the operating companies. He once called an emergency meeting of outside directors and demanded they allow him to fire the executive who was second in command because of a minor dispute. They reluctantly went along with his power play; however he had signed his own fate. Less than three months later he was ousted by the same group of directors.

Some leaders have an evolved ego in one area in their life and not in another. My observation of the late Richard Nixon was that as President he dealt effectively with many critical issues. For example, with the Soviet Union and China he was decisive, insightful . . . many people believe brilliant. However, in dealing with problems that related to him as a person, such as personal criticism by the press, he caved in.

**Have confidence in your leadership, while realizing that it will never be perfect**. You can develop an evolved ego (not easily offended or angered, good sense of humor) while having a burning, passionate desire to do well. It is possible to not take personal offense when criticized or when things go wrong--unlike someone with a more primitive ego (easily offended, easily angered, often exceedingly vain). Stick your neck out - ask for candid feedback about your performance from your boss, your peers, and your subordinates. It may enable you to make changes that will allow you to keep your job and continue moving upward.

There's a story about the CEOs of three high tech companies, which were direct competitors and simultaneously involved in a strategic alliance, who were drinking late one night and bragging to each other. The first said, *"History will show that I was the greatest high tech entrepreneur of the 20th century."* The second said, *"No, it is I who will be cited as the greatest high tech entrepreneur of the 20th century. I am sure of this because God himself told me so."* The third CEO responded, *"I never told you any such thing."* People who fit this profile often kneel at their own altar, flaunt their success, create high levels of resentment and frequently fail.

*The vast majority of conflicts between people at work are based on incompatibility caused most often by ego... not incompetence.* Cause your people to see themselves as working <u>through</u> you, not <u>for</u> you. Be willing to change or compromise . . . never paint yourself into a corner. It is very unlikely that your ideas will always be superior to others in your group.

An exceptionally brilliant executive lost a very senior job at one of the worlds largest companies because of his arrogance. He soon landed a senior position at another worldwide company and lost it for the same reason. He mistook intellectual brilliance as making everybody else inferior to him and he told them so regularly. He is now self employed as well as emotionally illiterate.

**Remember the difference between humility and humiliation.** Choose to be humbled by your losses, mistakes and failures. If you are humiliated by them, you handicap your ability to learn from your experiences. It is also likely you will brand yourself as a failure. Do not take successes and failures personally. **Your work is what you do. . . a person is who you are.**

Management consultant George Landis had a very challenging assignment with an automobile manufacturing plant. The goal was to get the plant manager and the head of the union, who were in a war of egos, to realize that their goals were the same. . .to make the plant profitable so that they could keep their jobs. After months of establishing trust and communications with each of them individually Landis was able to get them to talk. Once their egos were out of the way they worked well together and the result was a success for both management and labor. The plant that had been scheduled to be shut down because of multiple problems became the model plant for the entire firm (more than 100 plants).However, after Landis left and was not there to keep peace, the problem started again and the plant has returned to the endangered list.

## EVALUATE YOUR EGO

**Many otherwise intelligent people have serious difficulty working with others because of a primitive ego.** Their existence revolves around an attempt to guard the identity they project to the world. They spend a major portion of their energy defending themselves and their ideas--both to other people and to themselves. Because they have a strong, often overpowering need to prove themselves, these people often pile up notable achievements. However, their primitive ego acts as a barrier to long term success. People with primitive egos leave a trail of ruptured relationships behind them and are seldom invited to rejoin a group once they have left.

By contrast, people with evolved egos deal with themselves and others in a straightforward way. Acknowledging freely that they don't have the final answer to every question, they ask others for help and are open to ideas. Within their groups, they create trust, and they enhance the self-esteem of the members. They inspire others because they don't need to prove themselves superior or to get credit for every achievement.

**Remember - sometimes popular, always respected, exceptional leaders
strive for neither popularity nor agreement**

# THE BEGINNING OF ALL WISDOM IS TO STAND ASIDE

**Can an old dog learn new tricks? Yes! Is it possible to change your ego? Yes!
Recognize that your ego is always attempting to act in your best interest.** Create internal dialogue with your ego. Stand aside and observe your own behavior. You can be very successful in moving from a primitive to an evolved ego. It's surprisingly simple. Knowing why you are a certain way is the booby prize. Changing the way you are is the grand prize.

*The following is a test that will help you to evaluate your current ego handicap. If you would like an accurate assessment of your ego state, be sure to evaluate yourself as you are, not as you think you should be or would like to be.*

## EGO EVALUATION
**Scoring:  Never = 0    Sometimes = 1    Often = 2    Almost Always = 3**

_____ 1.  Is it frustrating when you cannot get people to do things your way?

_____ 2.  Do you often find it difficult to stay with arrangements you have made after the people involved seem less important?

_____ 3.  Do you enjoy being the "center stage" (center of attention)?

_____ 4.  Do you pride yourself on being able to outfox others?

_____ 5.  Are you someone who cannot be trusted?

_____ 6.  Do you feel rage when being ignored or not receiving first-class treatment?

_____ 7.  Do you often put people down behind their backs?

_____ 8.  Do you have difficulty enjoying your leisure time?

_____ 9.  Would you be embarrassed to be caught shopping in a store noted for low prices by someone you are trying to impress?

_____ 10. Do you drive a fancy car or live in an expensive home even if it strains your budget?

_____ 11. Are you afraid to admit to others that you are sometimes scared?

_____ 12. Do you have to look your very best when seen by other people?

_____ 13. Are you seduced by praise even when you sense it may be somewhat insincere?

_____ 14. If unable to express felt anger at someone because of his or her rank or position, will you explode at an innocent person?

_____ 15. Do you feel uneasy when someone is receiving what you consider to be undue praise?

_____ 16. Do you find it hard to pay a sincere compliment to someone who is doing better than you are at your line of work?

_____ 17. Do you often view people you meet as competitors or adversaries?

_____ 18. Do you feel superior or inferior to certain people?

_____ 19. Do you use people for your advancement even if it damages them?

_____ 20. Do you demand to be treated like royalty (even in unimportant matters)?

____ 21. Do you mind other people talking a lot about themselves?

____ 22. Do you talk a lot about yourself, your contacts, your accomplishments, etc.?

____ 23. Will you cover up something you have done poorly if you get the chance?

____ 24. Do you enjoy knowing that someone you dislike is having problems?

____ 25. Is it difficult for you to be gentle? Do you see it as a weakness?

____ 26. Do your actions make you a target of other people's anger?

____ 27. After scoring this questionnaire, will you discount the evaluation if you do poorly?

____ 28. Do you feel people are to be taken advantage of?

____ 29. Would you risk your life and perhaps the lives of your loved ones to prove your "courage," e.g., pursue a car recklessly on the freeway after it cut you off, to get even?

____ 30. Do you have a compelling need to prove yourself?

____ 31. Are you affected by other people's opinions of you in relationship to their importance and status?

____ 32. Do you believe that winning is the only thing, no matter what the consequences?

____ 33. Must you win even when enjoying your leisure time (golf, tennis, etc.)?

____ 34. Do you "validate" yourself even when your actions are not "valid," e.g., make lots of phone calls that are unnecessary to prove how important you are.

____ 35. Are you attracted to people who constantly reaffirm how important you are?

____ 36. Are you overly sensitive when hearing unflattering comments about yourself?


____ TOTAL SCORE-To determine your ego quotient, add up the numbers.


## Results:

(1) **0-25  You have reached a highly evolved ego.**   (3) **51-75  Your ego is in a primitive state.**

(2) **26-50  You have a reasonably evolved ego.**   (4) **Over 75 Your ego is highly primitive.**

Your total score is your "ego handicap." If your score is in categories (2), (3), or (4), you will benefit from implementing ideas to help lower your "ego handicap." In doing so, you will become more able to deal with yourself and others. If you have done poorly and are upset by the results, recognize that this is not something good or bad, but rather something that is, and that you can change it.


## THE 7 NEUROTIC NEEDS

**Evaluate yourself from  0 - 10 for the 7 most prominent neurotic ego needs.**
 They are:  1) *the need to procrastinate and/or avoid taking action,*  2) *the need to be liked,*  3) *the need to be needed,*  4) *the need to be treated fairly,*  5) *the need to be right,*  6) *the need to value judge and impose your values on others,*  7) *the need to resist reality.*  They can all be corrected with the new whole brain learning techniques.

# FACING MOMENTS OF TRUTH

The way you respond to a major crisis will determine whether you are an exceptional leader. While you may be effective most of the time, this *"moment of truth"* will reveal your leadership strengths and weaknesses. It will be the real measure of you as a leader.

## Moments of Truth: How will you handle yours?

THE BLUE CHIP ENTERPRISE AWARD, co-sponsored by the US Chamber of Commerce and *Nation's Business* magazine, is given annually to small businesses that have survived adversity of various kinds that would have destroyed most organizations. Having served as a judge for the Blue Chip Award for a number of years, I have been able to see a particular ingredient found in most organizations that survive extraordinary difficulties.
*The leaders refuse to accept failure. They make all required changes. . . often revamping the entire organization . . . in order to succeed. . .They simply will not give up!*
*They do not allow reversals to overpower their vision and hope for the future.*

**Here are examples of leaders who have faced their moment of truth and passed**

DAVID NEVENS and two partners formed a unique company in 1993. They assembled a group of top independent professional analysts that could audit and reduce the costs of utilities, telecommunications, freight, property and use taxes, and a number of other areas for organizations of all sizes. They charged organizations no fee and instead shared only in a percentage of savings they might find. They made immediate sales to a wide variety of organizations. However, the time it took to complete the auditing process and implement the changes meant that they received no income for seven to nine months after making a sale. The faster they grew the quicker they ran out of working capital. The other partners and all but one analyst quit. Their lawyer suggested closing the business. Nevens and the one remaining analyst, NEAL STEVENS, decided to find innovations that would allow them to remain in business. In just under a year (working other jobs at night to survive) they created proprietary software that analyzed clients energy bills more comprehensively than anyone in the industry. They also developed never before known strategies to help clients further reduce the cost of doing business. The company is now highly profitable and will soon be international.

**They faced their moment of truth and passed the test.**

JAKOB GRAY built a successful firm selling plastic auto parts to the Big Three automobile companies. After years of increasing sales, suddenly in an 18 month period, sales fell 38%. Upon evaluating the situation, he knew what had to be done. His sales force had succeeded by selling to auto firm purchasing agents. The car manufacturers, however, had moved to outside subcontractors to furnish the parts. His sales force could not make the adjustment. They didn't know how to sell to the new customers. Gray made training available to his sales people, but they were unwilling or unable to change. He had to replace the entire sales force, some long-standing personal friends. He did what was necessary, even though a number of the reps were vehement in their denunciation of him . . . calling him a traitor, etc.

**He faced his moment of truth and passed the test.**

TAYLOR MARMIE was one of five regional vice-presidents of a firm that reorganized and eliminated their jobs. They were all offered a job one level down. The others resigned in anger. Taylor realized that what had happened was not a personal attack. She knew it was done out of the firm's need to survive. She accepted the new job and continued to become an ever more valuable executive. Less than three years later she was the CEO.

**She faced her moment of truth and passed the test.**

GEORGE HUFF built a national financial services firm with over 150 employees. The firm sold a vast array of products through thousands of financial services executives and produced marginal profits. Huff re-thought his strategy and made bold changes. He sold the firm to start a new one. His new firm sells a small number of products through less than 60 financial services sales executives and employs only 5 people. It is very profitable.

**He faced his moment of truth and passed the test.**

DENNIS KENNA saw no future for himself as an administrative manager. He purchased a powerful personal computer and spent over 50 hours a week learning about computers, software and on-line technology. He persisted through long periods of extreme frustration and devastating disappointment. Finally, after more than 3000 hours of self directed study, he emerged as an on-line professional. Today he is an international award winning Webmaster on the World Wide Web with a number of clients in different industries and several countries.

**He faced his moment of truth and passed the test.**

JOHN GATTO was New York State Teacher of the Year in 1991. An exceptional teacher, he shortly thereafter came to an irrevocable decision . . . to resign. He concluded that the school system was designed to support the organization and not the students. Rather than teaching students to think on their own, he was required to teach a confusing curriculum of arbitrary justice, indifference to quality and dependency. He came to his moment of truth after 26 years as a teacher. He knew that reading, writing and arithmetic are so easy to learn that 100 hours will make a person proficient at all three. "School," however, had become an institution devoted to looking like it had valuable secrets that could not be found elsewhere. His decision left him unemployed. He will only work at a teaching job where the focus is on the students, not the organization.

**He faced his moment of truth and passed the test.**

STEVEN PIERSANTI was CEO of a publishing company within a large book publishing organization. He was directed to lay off a large number of his staff without reason or justification. Instead, he refused. He was fired and subsequently started a totally new kind of book publishing firm that allows authors to retain ownership of their books. His firm has published nearly 50 books in less than three years, including several best-sellers, and enjoys much more collaborative and mutually satisfying relationships with authors than do most publishing companies. He is a pioneer in changing the way books are published.

**He faced his moment of truth and passed the test.**

# YOU DO NOT HAVE TO WAIT FOR A CRISIS

All leaders experience moments of truth. Don't be caught off guard . . . prepare in advance.

**Fear of the known is at least as great as fear of the unknown:** Most major changes can be seen well in advance--for many leaders it is just too painful to face them until it is too late.  By resisting reality[+] they create their own failure.  **Procrastination can be fatal.**  Review your past moments of truth.  How did you handle them?  What did you learn?  Did you increase your ability to handle future ones?  If not, what changes will you now make?

*Be a "Change Vigilante".. Watch for early indications of the need for change. Advise your people to do the same.  Make all necessary changes as soon as soon as you see the need . . . to delay may be fatal.*

## *"Act As If Your Organization Is In a Crisis."*

A *Fortune* Magazine article, "Times Are Good: Create A Crisis"[++] tells how three top companies, leaders in different industries, dramatically improved the performance of their already highly successful firms by "creating a crisis."  The outcome was increased sales, reduced overhead and market share increase for all of them.

**Being in business today is like playing no rule baseball**.  Once you hit the ball, the opposing team can move the bases anywhere they wish . . . And they are doing it with ever greater speed.

Take immediate bold steps to improve the performance of your group in every way possible. Rehearse in advance of a crisis . . . it will prepare you for when a crisis does occur.  Create various simulations . . . you will be ready for moments of truth.  Practice . . . prepare . . . practice some more.  The astronauts each had to travel safely to the moon 300 times in the simulator before they qualified to actually go to the moon.

---

**Being successful in business today makes
being successful in business ten years ago look simple.**

**Being successful in business five years from today will make
being successful in business today look like child's play.**

---

[+] See *Seven Neurotic Blocks to Leadership,* by Christopher Hegarty.
[++] *Fortune,* June 28, 1993, page 123.

**The world is getting smaller . . . Competition is ever more ruthless.** Strategic decisions historically have relied on forecasts. They were arrived at by identifying and projecting past trends. Today, market realities change so fast that these methods are wholly inadequate. In the past, big companies could sell obsolete inventory to smaller companies in third world countries. Today with the astonishing increase of information available to everyone, the smaller company often knows the inventory is obsolete before the big company realizes it.

---

**Partnering with competitors?
Competing with partners?**

---

**Friend or foe . . . or . . . friend and foe.** Today, strategic alliances are being created between competitors. It is confusing, exciting and challenging to have a joint venture with an organization that you simultaneously compete against. What viewpoint do you have ?

*"Imagine having lunch with someone who is trying to eat your lunch."* To be successful at integrating these two seemingly opposing realities requires wholly new ways of thinking. It requires rethinking and unlearning... not all organizations or individuals will be successful at doing it. Make sure you are capable of it by establishing personal and professional strategic alliances with key people inside and outside of your organization. Intuitive intelligence is required. This **goes beyond culture shock . . . it is culture schizophrenia.**

## THE MO-BE-LE PRINCIPLE

Here's a new model for success - the Mo-Be-Le principle. Organizations and individuals are required to do mo-re . . . do it be-tter than ever before . . . with le-ss.

  *Mo-re -- Organizations and individuals are required to continuously increase their work output. As organizations downsize, leaving larger responsibility for those left, work must be ingeniously reorganized to be done more efficiently.*

  *Be-tter -- The quality of the work has to excel beyond any past level of performance. Even if your organization is number one in the eyes of the clients you serve, you are required to continuously improve the quality of everything you do, including the perception your clients hold of you. No matter how well you are now performing, continue to do it ever better on a permanent basis. **Keep raising the stakes.***

*Le-ss -- The increase in higher quality work has to be performed in less time, with fewer people and less resources. There are ways to do it . . . do it before your competitors do.*

Sounds daunting, doesn't it? There are many organizations[*] of all sizes that have proven their ability to excel in each of these areas for many years. Model your performance after them. Robert Waterman, author of *What America Does Right*, identifies two cardinal ingredients.

  *1) strategies that train and develop the skills of all the employees in an organization*

  *2) the ability to anticipate customer needs in advance of a problem*

**An average performing organization has a low probability of survival.** Do not be one.

---

[*] See *Leading Characteristics of Long Range Organization,* by Christopher Hegarty.

## WE ARE CAPABLE OF FAR MORE THAN WE REALIZE

*Dealing with change is a skill that can be learned. It is not possible to escape the future but you can be prepared to master it . . . no matter what it turns out to be. The future belongs to leaders relentlessly devoted to increasing the competence of all in their group.*

**It is the process of making changes necessary for survival that causes many leaders to become exceptional.** Organizations have improved their performance to levels that even the leader never dreamed was possible. **Individuals are capable of far more than they know.**

We honor people who run a 26 mile marathon . . . yet there are people in other parts of the world who run 70 to 100 miles non-stop on rough terrain without fancy shoes and do not think it is anything to talk about. In fact, there are runners in the United States who run an ultra marathon of 1300 miles in which they average 70 miles per day for 19 consecutive days.

**They are in peak physical condition but their training is more conditioning of the mind.**

To learn more, write: Ultra Marathon, 161-48 Normal Road, Jamaica, NY 11432.

**What is optimum performance?** It is the highest level known at any given moment . . . always subject to change. With the new skill training breakthroughs, all of us are capable of vastly higher levels of performance than we could have imagined five years ago.

# Rethinking and Unlearning

One of the most valuable skills is to unlearn ways of doing what you've learned to do. Here is a powerful exercise I developed 20 years ago that demonstrates unlearning. Use it with your group. Project the statement below on a screen and ask your group to do three things in silence. Caution them that each of the three are equal in importance. Have them 1) Read the statement below carefully and see what it means to them. 2) Count the total number of times the letter "F" appears in the statement. 3) Remember the words and in the order in which they appear (do not allow note taking).

THE MOST EFFECTIVE OF ALL HUMAN FEARS, WHICH PREVENT THE DEVELOPMENT OF ONE'S POTENTIAL, ARE THE FEAR OF FAILURE AND THE FEAR OF SUCCESS.

Have them stand while doing it and ask each person to be seated as soon as they complete all three tasks. When everyone is seated ask several people to explain what they got from the statement. (Then promise to come back to this in a minute). Next ask all the people who agree the total number of Fs is six to stand. (Remember this is all in silence.) Ask them to wager that they're right. The amount depends on the group. Then ask all those who agree the total is seven to stand up, then eight, then nine. Then ask those who agree the number is 10 to stand - and offer them a different bet. Ask them to wager that they can repeat the words in the exact order in which they appeared. You will find that those who counted to 10 most often paid no attention to your instructions to treat all three things equal in importance.

You will find that many of your people have differed on how many Fs there are. (If you haven't seen 10 yet go back and check until you are able to see them all.) Have them review in groups of four what they have all just experienced. Then return to a workshop on the power of fear of failure and the fear of success. It will be a valuable and insightful experience for your people.

**Many organizations and individuals continue to do things that are no longer necessary and in many cases are now counter productive.** In the days of manual typewriters the Qwerty keyboard was designed to slow the typist so that the mechanical keys would not jam. Today even though there is no need to limit speed 98% of all keyboards still employ the QWERTY. There would be a significant national increase in office productivity if the Dvorak keyboard (which has been available since 1932) that allows 79% more speed and 68% fewer mistakes was used. Billions of dollars in productivity are lost annually because of the reluctance to make changes even when they are well warranted.

**Stop doing things that make no sense .** Improve your competence by rethinking what you do and how you do it. Remember the old story of the pot roast. A newly married young man watched his wife prepare a roast for dinner. When she cut the end off the roast before putting it in the oven he asked, *"Why did you cut the end off the roast?"* She replied, *"That's the way my mother taught me to make a roast."* He called his mother in law and asked her. Her reply was identical *"My mother taught me."* He called his grandmother in law and asked her. Her reply was, *"During the Great Depression I couldn't afford a big enough pan to hold a whole roast."*

Here's another example. A friend came to my office and said, *"I need to see you now."* *"Please take no calls, "I need you to pay attention to a serious problem."* He then said, *"I love driving my fire engine red Porsche. I have received so many tickets that if I am caught once more I will be sent to jail. Help me figure out what to do."* I thought about it and said, *"I see three options ... 1) you can get someone to drive you."* He replied, *"I'd rather go to jail."* *"2) for $25,000 a year you can be named an honorary consulate to a poor third world country and be immune to tickets."* He smiled and said, *"I like that one a lot."* I then said, *"3) you can begin to drive within the speed limit."* He smacked his head and exclaimed *"Wow! I never thought of that."*
Watch out for QWERTYS, pot roasts and red Porsches. They come disguised in many ways!

The US faces a computer problem that is estimated will cost 800 billion dollars to remedy. Most computers will not recognize the year 2000. Unless corrected it could destroy our entire economy. The need to correct this has been well known for 40 years.

**Specifications and Bureaucracies Tend To Live Forever.** The US Standard railroad gauge (distance between the rails) is 4 feet, 8.5 inches. Why was that gauge used? Because that's the way they built them in England, and the US railroads were built by English expatriates. Why did the English people build them like that? Because the first rail lines were built by the same people who built the pre-railroad tramways, and that's the gauge they used. Why did "they" use that gauge then? Because the people who built the tramways used the same jigs and tools that they used for building wagons which used that wheel spacing. OK. Why did the wagons use that odd wheel spacing? Well, if they tried to use any other spacing the wagons would break on some of the old, long distance roads, because that's the spacing of the old wheel ruts. So who built these old rutted roads? The first long distance roads in Europe were built by Imperial Rome for their legions. The roads have been used ever since. And the ruts? The initial ruts, which everyone else matched for fear of destroying their wagons, were first made by Roman war chariots. Since the chariots were made for or by Imperial Rome they were all alike in wheel spacing. Thus, we have the answer to the original question. The US Standard railroad gauge derives from the original specification for Roman Imperial army war chariots which were made just wide enough to accommodate the exact back--ends of two war horses! Remember that when someone you're dealing with reminds you of the southern view of a northbound horse.

# CONCLUSION

## Leadership is an ongoing process

*"In a time of rapid change it is the <u>learners</u> who inherit the earth.
The <u>learned</u> are prepared for a world that no longer exists."*
*Eric Hoffer*

**You will make a difference.**  All leaders make a difference . . . some negative . . . some positive.  To be an exceptional leader requires relentless devotion to improving your skills.  Many exceptional leaders leave a magnificent legacy that lasts much longer than they live.

What is it to create a legacy?

*It is to plant a tree under which you will never sit. It is to look past your interests, your hopes and your lifetime... and put into motion changes that will be an indelible inspiration to those who follow.*

Countries, families and organizations grow or falter based on the strength of their leadership.  There are many skills necessary for leaders to succeed. The ones profiled in this program: *Vision, Execution, Inspiration, Drive, Ownership, and Empathy* are essential.

Remember:  **When a person stops learning he begins to die.**

> "Relentless *devotion* to improving your skills on a permanent basis is equal to or greater than any other single factor in becoming an exceptional leader."

Your skill at each can be continuously improved. While certain inherent strengths may make it somewhat easier for you to become an exceptional leader, the skills and competence necessary can and must be learned. There is a long running controversy over whether leaders are born or made.  Perhaps there is truth in both viewpoints.  Some gifted individuals seem to lead easily while others work diligently to become capable.  If I had to make a wager on which one of the leaders to bet on . . . I'd bet on the leader who diligently learned.  The optimum of course, would be the gifted leader who is continuously devoted to becoming ever more capable.

Take a long-term view. Do not be distracted by short-term interruptions. Be ruthlessly honest with yourself.  Do not resist reality (one of the seven neurotic needs that derails otherwise competent leaders).

*Be ever more <u>confident</u> about your ability to get the job done and simultaneously <u>humble</u> about your current level of competence. Deeply involve yourself in continuously learning new levels of competence. Always rethink. . . re-examine everything. . . relentlessly improve.*

*You can't get out of trouble doing what got you into trouble. Take risks, change your approach.*

If you have not had a major failure, chances are you will.  Many successful individuals have experienced failure, even despair, but continued to strive until they prevailed. Henry Ford and Walt Disney are among the numerous entrepreneurs who suffered massive business reversals, including bankruptcy, but did not allow anything to stop them from achieving their vision.

## TEACH YOUR PEOPLE THE DIFFERENCE
## BETWEEN LOYALTY AND CONFORMITY

*Exceptional Leaders knowingly establish high levels of trust and low levels of agreement with their people.* Exceptional leaders want everybody in the group to respectfully disagree with them and everybody else. They want every person in their group to be innovative and help lead the way to improved performance.

*Most other leaders unknowingly establish low levels of trust and high levels of agreement.* They expect people to agree with them and don't know how to measure trust let alone how to create it.

Teach your people the difference between loyalty and conformity. **Cause everybody to contribute to the group's success. Make them responsible and outspoken. They will compete and cooperate simultaneously and function** *as* **a team . . . not just** *on* **a team.**

> **Exceptional leadership** may require a high level of courage. When Peter Ueberroth accepted the leadership of the 1984 Olympics he decided to risk a bold new approach. Having just attended a course on *Ingenious Thinking* he realized that the traditional ways of doing things had resulted in massive financial losses. He developed and executed a radical new strategy that met with much resistance. His approach angered many people both inside and outside the Olympics. His life and the lives of his family members were threatened. His family dogs were poisoned. He persisted, however, and became internationally renowned because of the successful outcome of the 1984 Olympics . . . making hundreds of millions of dollars (where his predecessors lost hundreds of millions) that were used to further the cooperation of nations all over the world. While this is a dramatic example of the courage that is sometimes required to be an outstanding leader, even running a small organization may call for a great deal of courage.

## THE LEADER GETS THE RESULTS THE LEADER HAS THE RIGHT TO EXPECT.

What right do you now have to expect high levels of performance? Exceptional leaders continuously earn the right to expect ever higher levels of performance from themselves and all the people in their group. The leader does this by relentless devotion to a lifelong learning program designed to increasing all the competencies necessary to be an exceptional leader. Learn and apply what you learn. Keep getting a little bit better permanently and you will become an outstanding leader.

Let's take a last look at Warren Gregory. He continued up the ladder at his firm and then accepted the CEO position at another large firm. He always made it perfectly clear that the reason for his success was not exceptional ability of any kind. He succeeded because of a life-long devotion to improving his competence. His credo, *"I always want to get a wee bit better."*

He was a mentor to many . . . I know, because I had the privilege of working for him early in my business career. He caused me to believe I could succeed and then helped me develop the necessary skills. Like many others, I will value the impact of his leadership on me all of my life.

You write a self-definition of yourself by the way you spend your life. Leadership, like life, is not defined by where you started . . . it is defined by where you finish. It is exciting and rewarding to excel as a leader. It is a way to become someone you will be proud of.
 **You make a living by what you get and a life by what you give.**

What does history show us makes a leader great?  Commitment to improving.  Great leaders study, innovate and break free from traditional ways of thinking and doing.  The world faces many serious challenges.  It would be naive of us to underestimate the challenges we all face....It would be tragic to underestimate our ability to deal with them.

Keep your beliefs positive  because . . .

> *your **beliefs** become your **thoughts***
> *your **thoughts** become your **words***
> *your **words** become your **actions***
> *your **actions** become your **habits***
> *your **habits** become your **values***
> *your **values** become your **destiny***

*Mahatma Gandhi*

I was once on a  program with 14 other speakers, one of whom was Eric Hoffer.  The rest of us each spoke for an hour or longer.  Hoffer spoke for 12 minutes and was the most valuable  of all.  For years I quoted his closing comments in many of my presentations . .  then I heard a recording of his 12 minute speech and I discovered that he had not said anything remotely similar to what I was quoting him as having said.  I realized I was quoting what I had learned from his talk.   Here is the quote. *"People who invest themselves in becoming all they can become, and even more importantly, people who invest themselves in helping others become all they can become, are doing the most important work on earth . . .they  are helping to complete God's work.*

**The measure of your leadership is not determined by the size,
stature and public awareness of your work.**

You need not be famous or wealthy to be an exceptional leader. It is your value in whatever situation you are in whether it's raising a family, teaching in school or leading a country.  A single parent lovingly leading a family is at least as significant as an astronaut... an exceptional school teacher igniting the minds of students is at least as significant as the head of a worldwide business empire.

**THE ISSUE IS NOT *CAN YOU* BE AN *EXCEPTIONAL LEADER***

**. . . IT IS *WILL YOU?***

# About the Institute For Exceptional Performance

The Institute for Exceptional Performance has conducted more than 4000 speaking/training/consulting assignments for clients in over 30 countries.

The Institute offers training programs, consulting services, and published materials in the areas of leadership, change, stress, sales, and sales management, as well as other executive subjects.

Devoted to finding and using cutting edge breakthroughs in human competence, programs include:

- ◆ The Future Belongs to the Omnicompetent.
- ◆ Managing Personal & Professional Change.
- ◆ 7 Secrets of Exceptional Leadership.
- ◆ 7 Secrets to Beat Stress & Burnout.
- ◆ Eliminate Performance Fears - such as Public Speaking, Cold Call Selling, Fear of Failure, Fear of Success, and other fears that prevent high performance.
- ◆ Communication Training in Listening and Public Speaking.
- ◆ Ingenious Thinking: How to Jump Start Your Brain.
- ◆ Fiscal Fitness for Organizations

The Institute begins each assignment by researching the organization, its key challenges and its highest priorities. It then prepares a customized workbook to be given to each participant.

Our programs are highly interactive with maximum audience participation. Programs can no longer simply identify what changes people have to make and why. Today a program that identifies changes has to teach the skills necessary to make the changes.

Institute for Exceptional Performance
P.O. Box 1152, Novato, CA 94948  USA
Telephone (415) 892-2858
e-mail: leaders @cutting-edge.com

# WARNING . . . DO NOT STUDY ALL THE FOLLOWING MATERIALS

Choose carefully and focus only where you require insight.  If possible, get book reviews; they often cover the essential ingredients and can save you from reading the entire volume.

## General

Batten, Joe *Tough Minded Leadership,* Amacom, 1989.

Cooper, Robert K. and Sawaf, Ayman *Executive EQ,* Grosset/Putnam, 1997.

De Bono, Edward *The Act of Science and Success,* Little Brown, 1984.

Daley, H. Ray, Jr. *Up and In,* to be published 1996.

Follet, Mary Parker *Prophet of Management,* Harvard Business School Press, 1995.

Haggai, Tom *How The Best Is Won,* Thomas Nelson, 1987.

Hammer, Michael and Champy, James *Reengineering The Corporation,* Harper Business1994.

Hegarty, Christopher *How To Manage Your Boss,* Ballantine, 1984.

Hegarty, Christopher *Fiscal Fitness for Organizations,* Inst. Exceptional Performance, 1994.

Heider, James *The Tao of Leadership,* Bantam Books, 1986.

Hunt, Valerie *Infinite Mind:  The Science of Human Vibrations,* 1995.

Kelly, Dennis *The Six Steps to the Fountain of Youth,* Trineurogenics, Inc., 1997

Kriegel, Robert *If It Ain't Broke, Break It,* Warner, 1990.

Kriegel, Robert *Sacred Cows Make The Best Burgers,* Warner Books, 1996.

Munn, Michael  *Resonance: The Coming World Revolution in Business,* Inst. Excpt Prf ,1997

Raphel Murray & Neil Raphel, *Up the Loyalty Ladder,* Harper Business, 1995.

Renesch, John *New Traditions In Business,* Berrett-Koehler, 1992.

Schuster, Carpenter & Kane, *The Power of Open Book Management,* Wiley & Sons, 1996.

Shapiro, David Irving *You Must Not Let Them Con You! There's Too Much At Stake,* Mens Sana
    Fndtn 1994.

Waterman, Robert H. *What America Does Right,* Plume/Penguin, 1995.

## Vision

Cetron, Marvin *The Future of American Business,* McGraw-Hill, 1987.

Davis, Stan and Davidson, Bill *2020 Vision,* Fireside, 1991.

Harman, Willis and Rheingold, Howard *Higher Creativity,*  Jeremy P. Tarcher, 1984.

Pulos, Lee *Beyond Hypnosis.* Omega Press, 1990.

Russell, Peter and Evans, Roger *The Creative Manager,* MacMillan, 1992.

Talbot, Michael *The Holographic Universe,* Harper Collins, 1992.

## Execution

Bronstein, Howard and Ray, Darrell *Teaming Up: Making the Transition to a Self-Directed Team
    Based Organization,* McGraw Hill, 1995.

Campbell, Susan M. *From Chaos to Confidence,* Simon Schuster, 1995.

Covey, Stephen *The Seven Habits of Highly Effective People,* Fireside, 1984.

Decker, Bert *You've Got to be Believed to be Heard,* St. Martin's Press, 1992.

Hegarty, Christopher *Seven Neurotic Blocks to Leadership,* Inst. Excpt Prfm, 1979

James, Jennifer *Thinking in the Future Tense,* Simon Schuster, 1996

Kahaner, Larry *Competitive Intelligence,* Simon Schuster, 1996.

Kami, Michael, J. *Trigger Points,* McGraw Hill, 1988.

Meyer, Herbert E. *Real World  Intelligence,* Storm King Press, 1994.

Micklethwait, John & Wooldridge, Adrian *The Witch Doctors,* Times Business Books 1996

Mintzberg, Henry *The Rise and Fall of Strategic Planning,* New York:  Free Press,    1994.

Ueberroth, Peter *Made in America,* Morrow, 1985.

# Inspiration

The Bible.

Collier, Robert *The Secret Of The Ages,* Collier, 1924.

Dossey, Larry *Healing Words,* Harper Collins, 1993.

Frankl, Viktor *Man's Search for Meaning,* Revised Edition, Buccaneer Books, 1993.

Livingston, Sterling *Pygmalion in Management,* Harvard Business Review, Sept, 1988.

Marcic, Dorothy *Managing with the Wisdom of Love,* Jossey Vass, 1997.

Nightingale, Earl *The Strangest Secret,* recording, Nightingale Conant Corp.

Pearce, Terry *Leading Out Loud,* Jossey Bass, 1995.

# Drive

Assagioli, Roberto *The Act of Will,* Viking Press, 1974.

Hegarty, Christopher *7 Secrets to Beat Stress and Burnout,* Inst. Excpt. Prf, 1997.

Hill, Napoleon *Think and Grow Rich,* Fawcett Crest, 1960.

Katzenbach, Jon R. *Real Change Leaders* Times Business, 1995.

Nelson, Philip *Stress Analysis System,* IEP, 1993.

Pelletier, Kenneth *Sound Body, Sound Mind,.* Simon and Schuster, 1994.

# Ownership

Conner, Daryl *Managing at The Speed of Change,* Villard, 1993.

Newman, James W. *Release Your Brakes, The PACE Organization,* 1977.

Newman, Mildred and Berkowitz, Bernard *How To Take Charge of Your Life,* Bantam, 1977.

# Empathy

Abramms, Bob and Simons, George *The Questions of Diversity,* ODT Inc., 1995.

Bates, Marilyn and Keirsey, David *Please Understand Me: Character and Temperament Types,* Prometheus Nemesis, 1978.

Bretto, Charlotte and Hegarty, Christopher *How to Build Rapport,* Institute for Exceptional Performance 1991.

Hegarty, Christopher *Speak Easy to One or One Thousand* (a video film), Institute for Exceptional Performance, 1980, 1993.

Kantor, Jan *Inspiring People in the Workplace,* Island Press, 1992.

Mitchell, Arnold *The Nine American Life Styles,* Warner, 1988.

Nelson, Philip *Integrated Management Development System,* IEP, 1992.
*Position, Suitability Profile System,* IEP, 1993.

Richardson, Jerry and Joel, Marculis *The Magic of Rapport,* Avon Books, 1984.

Satir, Virginia *Peoplemaking II, Science and Behavior,* 1988.

For information on the Fox 40 whistle contact
Foxtron International, Inc.
20 Warrington Street
Hamilron Ontario
Canada L8E3V1
905-561-4040

# CHRISTOPHER J. HEGARTY

Christopher Hegarty is an international award-winning public speaker, best-selling author and management consultant. More than 400 of the Fortune 500 companies , numerous trade and professional associations, and many other large and small organizations in 31 countries have used him as a speaker/trainer/consultant. He is a member of The National Speakers Association Hall of Fame.

Clients include: *AAAA, APPLE, ASAE, AT&T, CHEVRON, CBS, CIBA-GIEGY, CIGNA, EDS, DUPONT, FTD, GENERAL ELECTRIC, GENERAL MOTORS, HEWLETT PACKARD, IAFP, IBM, INTEGRAL, INSTITUTE OF CERTIFIED FINANCIAL PLANNERS, INSTITUTE OF INTERNAL AUDITORS, INTERNATIONAL FOUNDATION OF EMPLOYEE BENEFITS, JOHNSON & JOHNSON, MDRT-TOP OF THE TABLE, MARRIOTT HOTELS, MOTOROLA, PG&E, PACIFIC BELL, PACIFIC MUTUAL, PRICE WATERHOUSE, PRUDENTIAL, RITZ CARLTON HOTELS, SHELL, SPRINT, WHIRLPOOL and YPO.*

Hegarty is the author of *The Future Belongs to the Omnicompetent, The New Rules: Managing Personal and Professional Change, 7 Secrets Of Exceptional Leadership, How To Manage Your Boss, 7 Secrets To Beat Stress and Burnout, How To Jump Start Your Brain, Leading Characteristics of Long Range Organization,* and *Financial Planning for CEOs.*

A principal of the Institute for Exceptional Performance and Christopher J. Hegarty & Associates, he has served as president of a national investment firm, founded an international mutual fund management company, and served as CEO of the International Center For Life Improvement, a foundation devoted to finding health and human competence breakthroughs.

He is Chairman of Advanced Resources Management, an award-winning high tech firm.

Hegarty earned a Doctorate in management education from the Creative Development Institute and has served on a special faculty of the University of Southern California.

As a consultant and advisor, Hegarty has had a variety of assignments including member of the President's Council at the American Institute of Management, advisor to the Governor of California, Strategic Consultant at Stanford Research Institute (SRI), and judge of the US Chamber of Commerce Blue Chip Enterprise Award.

*Nation's Business* cites Hegarty as one of the top management consultants in North America. *US News and World Report* considers him an expert on work and workaholism. References and articles about his work have appeared in more than 500 publications including *Forbes, Dun's Review, Industry Week, Government Executive, Entrepreneur* and *Readers Digest.* He has been listed in *Who's Who in Finance and Industry* and *Who's Who in the World.* He received the Legion of Honor award from the National Chaplains Association.

# PHILIP B. NELSON

Philip Nelson is a principal of IEP Consulting Group and has been a management consultant to major corporations, fast-growth companies and entrepreneurial ventures since 1974.

His consulting areas include: acquisitions and mergers, organizational change, organizational design and structure, program implementation and executive performance assessment. He also has expertise in succession planning, career development, team building, management development and in the selection and hiring process. He has worked extensively in startup companies and family businesses.

Dr. Nelson is well known for his work on leadership and on achieving superior managerial performance.

Clients include: FOX BROADCASTING, FOSTER FARMS, MILLIPORE, MATTEL, NATIONAL SEMICONDUCTOR, HEWLETT-PACKARD, CLOROX, GENERAL ELECTRIC, PFIZER PHARMACEUTICALS, AMERICAN BROADCASTING, UNISYS, THE URBAN LAND INSTITUTE, HEALTH CARE COMPARE and THE GOOD GUYS.

He was co-founder and co-director of the Vail, Colorado conference, "Stress Management and Human Illness" and was co-host on the television series, "Team at the Top."

Nelson's publications include: *The Integrated Management Development System*, IEP 1992; *The Position Suitability Profile System*, IEP 1993; *In Search of Mediocrity*, Woodside Press 1986; *The Stress Analysis System*, IEP 1993; *Recognizing and Redirecting Stress* (video and workbook), Knowledge Resources 1988; and *The Management Effectiveness Survey*, Interdatum 1986.

Before forming IEP Consulting in 1990, Nelson was a Senior Vice President with an international management and employment data company.

After receiving his Ph.D. in 1967 and before starting his corporate consulting career, Dr. Nelson worked in psychopharmacological and bioinstrumentation research. He taught at the University level and in medical residency programs. He also served as a director of a large and dynamic community psychiatric center.

# Planning Page

# Planning Page